THE ROMANCE OF TRISTRAN BY BEROUL AND BEROUL II

Student Edition and English Translation

The tragic tale of the lovers Tristran and Iseut was one of the most well-known themes of medieval literature. A story that is probably Celtic in origin, it was widely popular in the European Middle Ages and is found in numerous languages. One of its earliest appearances is the late-twelfth-century *Romance of Tristran*, written in Old French by Beroul. Based on the latest critical edition of the text, this volume features a new, accessible English prose translation of the poem, complete with explanatory notes. A valuable teaching resource for classes in medieval or comparative literature, *The Romance of Tristran by Beroul and Beroul II: Student Edition and English Translation* will be of interest to anyone fascinated by the origins of Arthurian legend or the literature of the high middle ages.

BARBARA N. SARGENT-BAUR is a professor emerita in the Department of French and Italian Languages and Literatures at the University of Pittsburgh.

T0339025

The Romance of Tristran by Beroul and Beroul II

STUDENT EDITION AND
ENGLISH TRANSLATION
BY BARBARA N. SARGENT-BAUR

UNIVERSITY OF TORONTO PRESS
Toronto Buffalo London

ISBN 978-1-4426-4986-6 (cloth)
ISBN 978-1-4426-2716-1 (paper)

Library and Archives Canada Cataloguing in Publication

Béroul, active 12th century
[Roman de Tristan. English]
The romance of Tristran by Beroul and Beroul II : student edition
and English translation / by Barbara N. Sargent-Baur.

Text in English; translated from the Old French.
Includes bibliographical references and index.
ISBN 978-1-4426-4986-6 (bound).   ISBN 978-1-4426-2716-1 (pbk.)

1. Tristan (Legendary character) – Romances.   2. Romances – Translations
into English.   I. Sargent-Baur, Barbara Nelson, translator   II. Title.
III. Title: Roman de Tristan. English.

PQ1537.A31 2015   841'.1   C2014-908044-1

University of Toronto Press acknowledges the financial assistance to its
publishing program of the Canada Council for the Arts and the Ontario
Arts Council, an agency of the Government of Ontario.

 Canada Council   Conseil des Arts
for the Arts   du Canada

University of Toronto Press acknowledges the financial support of the
Government of Canada through the Canada Book Fund for its publishing
activities.

Contents

Acknowledgments

I am much beholden to many scholars and editors who have, for over a century, wrestled with Béroul's fascinating and difficult text; my numerous debts to them are acknowledged in the Notes and in the Bibliography.

With deep gratitude I here take note of the professorial and indeed fatherly interest of Brian Woledge during my Fulbright year at University College London and for many years thereafter.

I thank Anne Melnyk for preparing the map of Cornwall, meant to assist the modern reader in following the comings and goings of the characters in this geographically specific narrative set in a location where several place-names have survived to our own time.

The task of preparing Béroul's *Roman de Tristran* for publication has been greatly lightened by the formidable technical skills, the attention to detail, and the meticulous proof-reading of Erich de Villiers.

The University of Pittsburgh has provided welcome material assistance in the form of a generous subvention from the Richard D. and Mary Jane Edwards Endowed Publication Fund in the Kenneth P. Dietrich School of Arts and Sciences. I greatly appreciate this support from the University of Pittsburgh, where I spent the whole of my academic career.

Preface

The story of Tristran and Iseut is one that enjoyed very wide currency in the European Middle Ages, and long afterwards. Its origins were most probably Celtic, and its early diffusion certainly oral; it doubtless pre-dated by a considerable lapse of time its first appearances in written form. Told and retold, added to and revised by professional story-tellers who had it in their repertory and carried it with them on their travels, it became one of the two best-known themes of European secular literature (the other being the quest for the Grail). The beginning of its peregrinations in oral form can only be guessed at before the twelfth century, when the first extant brief mentions and also substantial written texts began to appear; thereafter there is a sufficient body of literature and allusion to attest to its broad dissemination, from Italy to Iceland. Not all the evidence for the popularity of Tristranian motifs is literary; they also figure abundantly in the visual arts: tapestries, ivory coffers, paintings, and so forth.

Preserved literary treatments of the tale begin during the last third of the twelfth century with the German poet Eilhard von Oberge (the author of the earliest complete account extant). Full-length versions in French were composed in roughly the same time-period by the romancers Béroul and Thomas. The latter of these probably lived in England at the court of Henry II; the former may well have travelled in England. Both Béroul's and Thomas's narratives are incomplete[1] and must be supplemented from other sources. Parts of the early Tristranian material were expanded, and added to, in various languages, throughout the Middle Ages. The enormous development in French called the *Tristan en prose* made of Tristran a knight of the Round Table and entwined his story with the quest for the Holy Grail; this thirteenth-century amalgamation was much read and recopied in French. It was put into Italian as the *Tristano riccardiano* late in the fourteenth century and in the next century was incorporated into the *Tavola ritonda*. The *Tristan en prose* was read well into the Renaissance, when it was printed and so made far more accessible. Across the English Channel, the mid-fifteenth century saw the compilation of Sir Thomas Malory, *Le Morte Darthur*; this was preserved in manuscript, and was printed by Caxton in 1485. The part devoted to Tristran, from his birth to his death, bears the title *Sir Tristram of Lyonesse*; it is the fifth book of the *Morte* and furnishes about a third of the whole. There are some post-medieval treatments of the legend composed in various languages, but they are not numerous. One must wait until the Romantic era, marked as it was with the wide-spread enthusiasm for things medieval, to witness the serious study of the twelfth-century French poetic texts and also their edition and publication, beginning in the 1830s. Other expressions of renewed interest in medieval culture and its artistic and literary products, reinterpreted by and for the tastes of a later epoch, are manifest in a variety of areas. The 1850s, for example, saw the creation of *Tristan und Isolde* by Richard Wagner, still a staple of the operatic repertory.

To return to the twelfth century, by the middle of it the tale of Marc, Iseut, and Tristran, certainly Celtic in origin, was widely disseminated both in Britain and on the Continent, in French and in other languages as well. Marie de France, transplanted from her native land to England and roughly coeval with the person(s) responsible for the extant *Roman de Tristran*, claims in her brief "Lai du Chevrefoil" to have heard numerous recitals of the story of Tristram and the queen, and also to have seen it in writing.[2] In his first extant romance, *Erec et Enide*, her contemporary Chrétien de Troyes allots one line in passing to *Isolz la blonde* and two to Tristran's slaying of the *Morhot* in the *isle Saint Sanson*. In his second narrative, *Cligés*, he repeatedly alludes to Marc, Ysalt, and Tristran; and in the Prologue thereto he cites, in a list of "works by the same author," a *conte* "del roi Marc et d'Ysalt la Blonde." This account has unluckily not been preserved.[3] Chrétien's contemporary the Middle High German poet Eilhart von Oberge treated in his *Tristrant*, and at length, much of the story recounted by Béroul; it is generally assumed that both romancers drew from a common source, and represent the *version commune* of the tale. (The *version courtoise* is represented by Gottfried of Strassburg and Thomas of England.)

As for the author we are seeking at present, I opt to refer to him as Béroul, twice named in the first part of the text. This, though, is a matter that has been often and lengthily debated by careful scholars, and it reduces to three chief possibilities. The romance may be the work of two poets both treating materials available in England and France, the second of them picking up within a quarter-century or so from where the first one had left off; he did not revise but continued the unfinished copy he had before him, and also interpolated new episodes into the existing narrative. This is the view towards which I am inclined.[4] Then again Bérous/Béroul may be the creator of an earlier text now lost, seen by a nameless person who took it to be the authentic account of the story, and who reworked it (expanding as he went on) into the copy of which we possess the long extant fragment. A third possibility is that the *Berous* twice named in the text, in the third person, may be credited with as much of the whole poem as has come down to us (having coyly concealed his identity for reasons best known to himself). The passages in question are these:

Story-tellers say that they drowned Ivain; they are crude drowned Ivain; they are crude and do not know the story well; Béroul has it better in his memory. Tristran was too noble and courtly to kill people of such a sort. (1265–70)	Never, since the time when they took to the woods, did two people drink so much of such a draught. Nor, as related by the story there where Béroul saw it written, did any persons love each other so much or pay for it so dearly. (1787–92)[5]

These portions of the text contain two noteworthy points. One is that the tale of Tristran and Iseut was already being circulated in French. Story-tellers (*contëor*) were doing this, but from memory, inaccurately (Tristran and his tutor and companion Governal, antecedents of the first "they" in line 1265, do not, in Béroul's account at any rate, kill the lepers' chief, Ivain), and with touches of which *Berous* (who has heard them) strongly disapproves. Such bungling raconteurs are merely *vilain*, incapable of appreciating the hero's qualities; Tristran was too noble to drown (or simply "slay") the lepers to whom Marc had handed over his queen as punishment for adultery. To make matters worse, such an error of detail implies that in general these story-tellers are less than familiar with the *estoire*, which *Berous* remembers better than they. Some five hundred lines after this bit of self-promotion, the narrator returns to the theme of the "true story" and his own superior acquaintance with it. Now we encounter the claim that never did two people partake of such a draught (sc. pleasure mingled with pain), or love so intensely, or pay for it so dearly. Not only does the *estoire* say this, but Béroul has actually seen the tale in writing (unlike, he implies, his rivals, who are limited to what they may or may not recollect from listening to each other and sharing their ignorance).

Hence the two passages in which *Berous* names himself function to authenticate, and thus promote, his retelling of the *estoire*. We are confronted with a medieval commonplace: the author of a particular text prides himself or herself not on originality but on fidelity to the "true story," at the same time claiming to have presented this well-known, and basically worthy, material more accurately and competently and seemingly than other relaters have done and may currently be doing. He also manages to insinuate that people of taste will prefer his version to those of his rivals: the well-known ploy of *captatio benevolentiæ*.

There remains, though, the problem of a confused and confusing passage, 2754–64, offering information that clashes with what precedes and also what follows. There is a discrepancy with respect to the number of Tristran's enemies remaining after one of them has been killed; this fact has been taken as supporting a change in narrator, i.e., of author.[6] Alternatively, the original author may have forgotten what he wrote in the earlier half of the poem, or changed his mind but neglected to resolve the ensuing contradictions. One author or two? I have opted to refer to the writer of the first part as "Béroul" and his successor as "Béroul II" when making the distinction seems indicated.

The historical Béroul(s) can be glimpsed through his/their period, language, what the dialect implies as to geographical origin and that of family, his/their general culture, and his/their knowledge of the areas providing the settings for the story to be told. Certainly he/they lived in the second half of the twelfth century, at a time when oral literature of all sorts was rising to the dignity of being preserved in written form in some of the European vernaculars. His/their formation is not clerical, but it perforce reflects the ambient culture shaping the thought and behaviour of all strata of his society. Here the strongest influence was the Church with its dogma, organization, rites, calendar, and moral instruction, as received by the laity (primarily illiterate) with varying degrees of comprehension. So pervasive was its influence that even tellers and writers of stories meant as entertainment rather than instruction took for granted its central role in the lives of all, and did not risk boring their potential audiences with what everyone knew from childhood. The same consideration obtains with regard to the structures and obligations of secular society. That this last was hierarchical was taken for granted; the monarch, his immediate family, the great magnates who owed them honour, advice, and knightly service as required, and so on down to sub-vassals, artisans, farmers, men-of-all-work, and serfs – all except for outlaws had their place, and knew their place. Within each class, and among all classes, there was a web of mutual duties and obligations familiar to all. It was not in need of being spelled out except in abnormal situations such as a refusal of vassals to obey their lord, or a flagrant case of infidelity on the part of a married noblewoman. (A husband's straying was treated more indulgently.)

This well-established ecclesiastical and social stratification forms the background of the whole romance; it is the norm against which actions in the real world, and consequently in that of fiction as well, were measured by observers of events and also by hearers and readers of tales offered as "true." The story of Tristran and Iseut, in its various tellings, would have been received by a medieval audience differently from the ways in which many of our contemporaries, accustomed to the primacy of individual autonomy in most spheres of life and particularly in that of sexual attraction and behaviour, would respond to it. An effort needs to be made, and is worth making, to consider the tale as a twelfth-century man or woman would have done, someone whose reactions any writer (naturally hoping to please) would have had an interest in anticipating, and in guiding. From that standpoint, we see that the romance is structured both by love and by the tensions generated through a major threat to the social order. Iseut is not just Everywoman but a queen; if she is unfaithful to her husband she is in violation of her marriage vows made before God and man and confirmed by the Church as a sacrament. She is also transgressing against the accepted norms of the society in which she lives; in short, she is guilty of treason at the highest level, as is her lover. (That they are well aware of this is demonstrated by the great care they take to deny and conceal and even justify their transgression.) This is the ground of the complaint repeatedly made by three of Marc's great barons. The situation is scandalous, politically as well as morally. If the king is unaware of this, it is their obligation, as they repeatedly remind him, to inform and counsel him. If he does know of it, and nevertheless does nothing to cope with the situation and execute justice on the offenders, he is derelict in his duty (and, by implication, unworthy to command their services).[7] They do at one point temporarily withdraw from the royal court to their own strongholds (3143–7), and will cause trouble for their sovereign if the matter is not settled.

Béroul labours to distract the attention of his hearers or readers away from the objective legalities of the situation and towards the character and motivation of the three denouncing barons. They enter the narrative under the handicap of a pre-emptive strike on the part of the author: they are first mentioned, then branded as *felons* than whom the audience has never seen worse (581–2). Oddly enough, Béroul straightaway not only informs us of their decision to leave the court unless Tristran is sent away but also supplies in the authorial voice the factual grounds for their resolution: they have actually witnessed Tristran and the queen misbehaving in the garden and often in Marc's very bed during his absences. The barons will put up with this no longer, for they are sure that Marc knows of this wickedness and condones it (613–17). They present the king with an ultimatum: he must choose between keeping Tristran with him and having them and their associates stay at court. Yet far from being brought before us as disinterested upholders of morality and of duty to one's superiors, they are shown as animated by personal resentment against their king's nephew. Tristran had succeeded in defending the realm against a dangerous foreign aggressor (the Morholt), whereas they had revealed themselves to be fearful or unwilling or incompetent to do so; and this was common knowledge.

It is an accident of the manuscript's history that we first hear of the hero's adversaries in the speech of Iseut that begins the preserved fragment: in it she twice describes them as *felon* (26, 132), well aware that Marc is present and listening up in a tree. Here this is her own subjective judgment; but the term *felon* (noun and adjective) is also liberally sprinkled by the narrators through the text (lest the hearer or reader be inclined to form an independent opinion?). The hostile barons are invariably depicted as generally evil and specifically jealous of Tristran's knightly prowess and of his privileged position at court.

As for Tristran, the poet leaves no doubt of his love for the queen and of the physical nature of that love. (How it is that Iseut, with both husband and lover, never becomes pregnant is a matter for which no explanation is ever offered, here or in other accounts.) Béroul is solidly on the side of the lovers and against their detractors, as are most of Marc's subjects, who view Tristran as the national saviour and protest strongly and unanimously against the pronouncement of a death sentence on the guilty pair (827f.). That they are indeed guilty of adultery is a matter that the poet does not leave to the reader's imagination. Here again, though, Béroul is careful to guide the response of his audience. It is not the fault of Tristran and Iseut that they became lovers. Circumstances not of their choosing lie behind their passion (which antedated

Iseut's marriage). In Béroul's fragment these factors are not presented sequentially.[8] What the two of them repeatedly assert is that they were not responsible for the beginning of their illicit relationship; it was "li lovendri[n]s, li vin herbez" (2138) that overcame them. This had been brewed by Iseut's mother with the best of intentions, to ensure the love of her daughter and her royal husband-to-be. It was by accident that Iseut's maid, rather than keeping it for the marriage, served it on ship-board to her mistress and to Tristran (the latter having sailed to Ireland to fetch Iseut as bride for his uncle and lord). As for the hero and hero-ine, they had no inkling of what they were about to drink. Thus it was a concatenation of events, and mistakes not of their making, that were at the source of their mutual passion. Regret it as they might, suffer for it as they must, they were powerless to resist it. The clearest and longest statement of their own perception of their case comes in the visit they pay to the hermit Ogrin (1362–1423), to whom chance brings them during their forest wanderings. He exhorts them to repent and confess, but in vain. From each of them he receives only an explanation and an excuse: we love each other only because of the potion we both drank. "Ce fu pechiez" (1415). The expression has no moral force but merely states an attitude: it's too bad. Unrepentant and unabsolved, they return to their life as outlaws and savages.

Eventually the day and the very hour come round when the three-year term of the potion expires. Each of the lovers, during a brief sepa-ration, suddenly sees things differently (2147–2216). Each regrets the courtly, comfortable, civilized life that they have left behind for the dangers and hardships of their forest existence. The memories of rank, privilege, deference, luxury, activities befitting their station, fine apart-ments, and clothing come flooding upon them. First each expresses in turn an altered way of understanding the situation, and a drastic change of heart. Then, without transition, their monologues are suc-ceeded by a dialogue (2217f). They agree to ask pardon of King Marc on the grounds that (1) the potion was the cause of their misconduct and (2) no affection between the two of them would henceforth be of a kind to bring dishonour upon him. Tristran is to seek advice as to how he may be reinstated in his uncle's good graces, defend himself in combat against anyone accusing him of dishonourable doings with the queen, and serve the king in his wars. As guarantor of his and their amendment, Iseut recommends recourse to Ogrin. Kneeling at his feet, Iseut vows that at present her love for Tristran, still strong, is love for a friend, without a sexual component. The hermit is impressed by the lovers' resolution to cease sexual relations[9] to the point of assuring them

of God's forgiveness (2345–50). As for the judgment of man, it is sometimes convenient "to lie a little, fittingly" (2354). Ogrin, persuaded of
the lovers' remorse and confident that God will accept it, composes a
letter to Marc in which Tristran offers to return his queen to him and
re-enter his service if this is acceptable. He will meet in combat anyone
who might raise the subject of an illicit relationship; he had carried Iseut
off, true, but only to save her from the stake. (Ogrin knows full well that
no one would risk accepting Tristran's challenge, 2366–73.)

It is noteworthy that Ogrin's letter as proposed to Tristran and
accepted by him (2360–2409), with a concluding direction as to where
Marc's reply is to be left, is shorter than the letter as read aloud to the
king and his barons by the royal chaplain (2553–2618). The two commu-
nications also do not correspond in all details. In both versions Tristran
offers to do combat with any of Marc's barons who might accuse the
queen of infidelity, and promises to serve the king faithfully if permit-
ted; if not, he will leave the kingdom and offer his service elsewhere.
Moreover, in the second version he reiterates his role in bringing Iseut
to Marc's kingdom, killing the dragon and so winning Iseut for Marc.
He also asserts that not long after that marriage, tale-bearers began to
spread slander, telling lies about himself and the queen (2566–7). He
is now ready for judicial combat to prove their innocence and loyalty.
If reconciliation with the king is not possible, he will return Iseut to
her own country. The barons' response to this ultimatum is to advise
Marc to take back the queen and to dismiss Tristran for a year or two
(2671). This decision, communicated to Tristran, clears the way for the
parting of the lovers at the Mal Pas, the reunion of Marc and Iseut, her
reintegration into society (marked by a joyful royal progress into the
city of Lancïen), and her acceptance by the Church. Closure has been
accomplished. Yet the romance does not end here. The lovers will be
physically separated, but by no great distance. When the time of parting approaches they exchange pledges of love (2695–2732, 2777–2812).
Iseut begs Tristran to leave his hunting-dog Husdent with her, as a reg-
ular reminder of its owner; and to him she presents in turn a seal-ring,
which is to authenticate any message he may send to her. As soon as
she sees it she will do his bidding (2797–2802). Tristran, far from going
off to Galloway as promised, will on Iseut's advice take shelter with
Orri the forester, and they have made careful plans to remain in communication. When they join the royal train, Tristran restores Iseut to the
king and immediately solicits the opportunity to justify the two of them
through judicial combat. The issue at stake will be the innocence of their

relationship, not only at present but from the beginning. Yet Tristran is aware of having wronged the king, and so wears his halberk (2772–4); hence the request he makes of Marc as soon as they are within speaking distance is arresting, to say the least. Before him and all the men of his land he requests the opportunity to exculpate himself and the queen through some sort of judicial combat. His claim is that they had never had an improper relationship with each other, not for a single day, and that Marc had been brought to believe a lie (2853–9). Tristran had been accorded no trial to settle the matter before the two of them had fled for their lives. Now is the opportune moment to demonstrate the truth of the affair. Defeat for Tristran would be a sure sign of guilt, he acknowledges, and would justify his execution; if he should emerge unscathed from the combat, he begs Marc to retain him in his service or else he will go off to another kingdom. The three hostile barons argue strongly against Marc's keeping Tristran with him; it would cause a general scandal and reflect badly on the king. Let Tristran absent himself for a year; they propose that this space of time would permit the king to test his wife's fidelity (2893–2906). (Since she had not been suspected of adultery except with Tristran, she will predictably behave herself in his absence; no one in the romance mentions this obvious fact.) Béroul (or his source), though, is not through with the story.

It is the three *felon* who again upset the equilibrium established by Tristran's departure from the court and the queen's return to it. Before a full month has elapsed (3031), on a hunt with Marc, they take up their old refrain: if the queen has misbehaved, she has never denied it, and this is damaging to the king's honour. If lies are being told concerning her, she has the obligation to contradict them (as the barons of the land have repeatedly requested) or else to quit the kingdom (3054). In exasperation the king threatens to recall Tristran, and no later than the next day (3078–9). The three troublemakers, terrified, resolve never to raise the subject again, as they promise him while protesting their loyalty and good intentions. To no avail; they are banished from the land, and withdraw to their own castles (3147).

Stasis of a sort is re-established: Marc trusts Iseut, confident that Tristran is far away. Yet his anger is alarmingly apparent – not, it emerges, with Tristran, but with the *felon*. Marc assures the queen that Tristran will soon return and avenge him on the three of them. Once again judicial combat seems to be on the horizon, and with predictable results. At this juncture Iseut unrolls an elaborate plan under the guise of asking her husband's advice. She proposes to make a formal denial concerning her relationship with Tristran, and not merely before Marc's household and the three felons (who would never be satisfied thereby, 3233–8). She wants another court to witness her exculpation: that of King Arthur and the great figures of his household. They could be relied upon to come to her aid after witnessing her oath-taking, if it should become necessary. The swiftness and efficiency with which she takes charge of the matter leaves her husband nothing to do but agree (3277). Arthur and a hundred of his household knights are to be invited to come to her formal exculpation, as well as the whole population of Cornwall. Arthur's court will be summoned – by Iseut's own messenger, Perinis. This squire is dispatched with further instructions: he must not fail to make a detour on his errand to Arthur in order to seek out Tristran, still sheltering with Orri the forester. Through Perinis, Tristran is informed of the coming ceremony in Arthur's presence; date and place are named precisely, his disguise and behaviour prescribed in detail. On goes Perinis to Arthur's court with the lengthy oral message from the queen concerning the coming event with details of where and when; to this he receives an affirmative and enthusiastic answer. He carries it back to Iseut, to whom he gives an account of his whole expedition (3559–61). The author, though, takes care not to inform either the future participants in this drama, or his readers or hearers, of how Iseut means to exculpate herself once and for all before the two assembled courts.

At this point there is a notable slowing-down of the narrative. On the day before the oath-taking the witnesses begin to gather near the Mal Pas. Tristran, costumed as a begging leper, emerges from his hiding-place with Governal, whom he instructs as to what equipment he is to bring to the ford (including his lance with Iseut's pennon attached), and how he is to disguise Tristran's well-known steed. He is to conceal himself at the ford and there await his master. The latter establishes himself on a mound near the marshy shore and solicits alms of all comers (3627–62). Many knights, attempting to cross over, come to grief in the marsh (owing in part to false directions given them by the "leper"). In one way or another, both Arthur and Marc and their retinues manage to get across. Iseut arrives with Dinas, Marc's seneschal, who is a friend of the lovers, ascertains that Tristran is there as instructed, and dismounts. By now the only persons on the near side of the Pas are Iseut, Dinas, and the "leper"; all the others become spectators. Having their undivided attention, she whips her palfrey, which also gets to the other side. Dinas warns her about spoiling her splendid clothes by trying to cross by the wooden walkway; then, guessing her intention from her wink, goes off to a different ford. Now queen and "leper" remain on an otherwise empty stage. Peremptorily she commands him to carry her across, on his back, by using the walkway. She mounts "like a boy" (3931) and so reaches the other bank with clothes clean, and is now able to take the oath that is to exonerate her once and for all. As for the "leper," he disappears unrewarded and unthanked, rejoins Governal (who has brought horses, arms, and armour), and becomes a knight once again (although in disguise). Mounted and armed, the two of them burst upon the Blanche Lande and engage in some impromptu jousting. The main purpose of this is to reassure Iseut of his presence (he carries on his lance the pennon she had given him). He and Governal also manage to disable one of Tristran's enemies and kill another before vanishing.

On the following day begins the climactic scene of Iseut's formal disculpation. Now several of the main threads of the narrative are tied together: that of the stratification of society as represented by loyalty owed by some members to others (e.g., by a queen to her husband, and by vassals to their overlord); that of oaths sworn before God and man (4105–8, 4159–66, 4201) as reliable guarantors among human beings; and that of the Church in its various functions as the proper supervisor of tests of truth in difficult cases. On this solemn occasion it is not only God and the living who are invoked; many saints gone to their reward are also recruited as silent witnesses. Throughout Cornwall every sort of reliquary has been emptied and its contents brought before the tents of the two kings, so that Iseut will be able to swear upon them. Arthur, acting as master of ceremonies, first admonishes Marc for his credulity in believing rumours and promises that anyone who again accuses Iseut of adultery will have him to deal with. Then he specifies the substance of the oath the queen will take before the assembled witnesses, high and low (4160), and the Heavenly King: never did she and Marc's nephew share, to the slightest degree, a dishonourable love. The crucial moment has come. Iseut, flanked by Marc and Arthur, offers two refinements to the oath as proposed. She will swear not merely upon the relics spread out before her; she invokes those that are not there, all of them, throughout the world. Secondly, going beyond the suspected and proposed Tristran, she undertakes to affirm that no man has ever been between her thighs except King Marc, her spouse – and, of course, the leper who carried her across the ford on the previous day, in the sight of them all. Now the assembled witnesses, speaking as one, declare themselves satisfied, and repeat the essential terms of her defence. Gawain,

Arthur's spokesman, warns the three felons never again to speak of the matter; from wherever he may be, if summoned, he will come to act as the queen's champion (4235–46).

After this brilliant and lengthy episode (it takes up nearly a quarter of the preserved romance), what follows must seem anticlimactic, in part because it breaks off inconclusively. Iseut thanks Arthur for his support; Arthur begs Marc never again to believe a scoundrel concerning his queen. The kings and their courts separate, Marc's marital harmony and the order of his realm have been reestablished, the accusing barons have been silenced, Tristran has disappeared. The two kings and their courts go their own ways.

The poet, though, has more to relate.[10] Tristran's absence is only a ruse; he lurks in the vicinity of Marc's palace, and has been detected by someone hoping to rise in the world. This spy goes to the three *felon* with an offer to show them Tristran, and in the royal chamber, if they make it worth his while. The bargain is struck, the observation post and access to it are described; the trouble-makers are to keep watch for three days. As it happens, a clandestine visit by Tristran to Iseut has been arranged for the next day, in Marc's announced absence. Godoïne is chosen as eyewitness to the activity to be observed in the royal chamber. At night Tristran sets out from his hiding-place (at Dinas's residence?), and on his way encounters two of his enemies, killing one but losing track of the other. The latter, Godoïne, makes it to the peep-hole described by the spy and is installed there, watching but invisible, when Tristran appears with his trophy of his dead opponent's braids. Iseut, having noticed the shadow at the window, gives Tristran no normal reception but begins to chat about archery and in particular how Tristran goes about stringing and drawing his bow. Much puzzled but alert, he obligingly demonstrates this, glances towards the window curtain, sees the shadow of a head, prays a most inappropriate prayer,[11] and lets fly his ready arrow. Being Tristran, he does not miss. His enemy tumbles down dead, no shriving-time allowed.

And here the romance breaks off.

This account of the lovers of Cornwall is in French, which, of course, was the language of royal and noble life both in France and in England after the Norman Conquest and hence was employed in secular writing aimed at courtly patronage in either country. For the most part, the spelling and rhymes of both narrators are consonant with the standard literary language (*Francien*) of the latter part of the twelfth century, while also reflecting the speech of southern or southeastern Normandy, where presumably they were born. The very frequent cultural contacts between France and Norman England assured that a writer and/or story-teller from the one country could count on being understood in cultivated circles in the other, and might make a career on either side of the Channel. As for the settings of the tale, one can take it that the abundant references to specific places in Cornwall, to their character and their siting relative to natural features and each other, strongly suggest that one or both authors spent some time travelling in that part of the island, talking to its inhabitants and picking up local place-names and lore. The evocations of other areas in Britain are by contrast rather more general, even mythical (e.g., the trip undertaken by Perinis to find King Arthur, a quest during which he is promised a sight of the Round Table – a promise that the poet subsequently neglects to fulfil).

The particular features of the language of *Tristran* have been studied by philologists for over a century. The task is a challenging one, owing to multiple factors. Like other writers of French narrative in the latter half of the twelfth century, Béroul and Béroul II composed in verse and specifically in rhyming octosyllabic couplets, a medium that imposed formal constraints on narrative flow and also on vocabulary and syntax. This last element in the *Roman de Tristran* is frequently subject to unorthodox handling; many infractions of the two-case system (and there are indeed very many, some attributable to the careless scribe but others to be laid at the poets' own door) can only be explained by the constraints of metre and rhyme. One might offer in the authors' defence that, after all, their verses were meant to be read aloud to an audience, one hungry for entertainment and perhaps not inclined to be critical; they were not intended for grammarians and editors.

This volume is addressed to the non-specialist reader, one having a broad interest in the secular literature of medieval Europe and in world literature generally. The topics that attracted the audiences of medieval story-tellers, that the latter were happy to recite and rework, and that scribes sometimes committed to writing are of broad appeal beyond the period and the linguistic areas of their origin.

NOTES

1 Béroul's account is preserved in one source, f.fr. 2171 of the Bibliothèque nationale de France (BnF) in Paris. It lacks both beginning and ending; the preserved part (4485 lines) is sequential, albeit damaged. Thomas's

account is fragmentary; only eight passages (3146 lines) remain, scattered in five manuscripts of which three survive. For Béroul's text, see the Critical Edition. NB: illegible lines and words are here indicated by suspension marks; resolutions conjectured by other editors and by me appear between square brackets.

2 Marie does not specify on which side of the Channel she heard and read this tale. It was, she asserts, Tristram himself who had composed the *lai*, words and music alike. He did so to commemorate his joy at seeing his beloved (and also what he had previously written to her?), following their clandestine meeting in a forest between Marc's unspecified base and Tintagel. In his first preserved romance, *Erec et Enide*, Chrétien de Troyes repeatedly alludes to Marc, Ysalt, and Tristran and in his Prologue cites (line 5), in a list of "works by the same author," a *conte* "del roi Marc et d'Ysalt la blonde"; it has unluckily not been preserved. The Middle High German poet Eilhart von Oberge treated in his *Tristrant*, and at length, much of the story recounted by the French romancer; it is generally assumed that he and Béroul drew from a common source.

3 Chrétien de Troyes, *Erec et Enide*, lines 424, 1246–7; *Cligés*, line 5 et passim.

4 The dual-author thesis was announced by Ernest Muret in the title of his first edition (1903): *Le Roman de Tristan par Béroul et un anonyme, poème du XIIe siècle*; see his *Introduction* IV, *Les auteurs*, lxiii–lxxii. The thesis was reaffirmed by Guy Raynaud de Lage in "Faut-il attribuer à Béroul tout le Tristran de Béroul?" in *Moyen Age* 64 (1958) and 70 (1964). T.B.W. Reid, in "The *Tristran* of Beroul: One Author or Two?" *Modern Language Review* 60 (1965), refers to Beroul I and Beroul II. In the Introduction to his 1992 edition of *The Romance of Tristran*, Stewart Gregory examined (pp. xxiii–xxvii) the evidence advanced in favour of the dualist hypothesis and cautiously concluded that the preserved text is the work of a single author.

5 The English version is taken from the present edition.

6 See note 4. I opt to use "Béroul" and "Béroul II" when a distinction between the authors seems indicated.

7 One might conjecture that underlying the barons' consistent opposition is a factor implied but left unspecified in the preserved fragment of the romance, yet one that, mentioned or not in the complete text, might well have occurred to a twelfth-century hearer or reader: if King Marc should die without a son to succeed him, it would be normal for another close male relation to be in line for the throne. This claimant would be Tristran, Marc's nephew, who as his heir would become their suzerain. In the roughly contemporaneous treatment by Eilhard von Oberge, which survives complete in three manuscripts, the matter is raised and spelled

out: Mark is so fond of his nephew Tristrant that he refuses to marry; Tristrant will be as a son to him and inherit the kingdom.

8 For material in the common source(s) preceding the text at hand, one must turn to Eilhard.

9 Iseut, although unrepentant, promises Ogrin that in future the relationship will no longer be carnal but purely amicable, 2323–30.

10 Béroul II, seemingly enamoured of his tale and reluctant to end it, tries to have things both ways: the potion has lost its power after exactly three years, yet the lovers have resumed their clandestine meetings and love-making (if this is the meaning of the rare word *orlois* in 4338) during Marc's absence.

11 As to Christ's sacrifice and Tristran's wished-for revenge: Braet/Raynaud de Lage alone have signalled the shocking nature of this association of ideas, 4463–71.

CORNWALL

Scale of Miles

0   5   10

THE ROMANCE OF TRISTRAN BY
BEROUL AND BEROUL II

Translation

. . . .   1a
so as to give no sign of anything.
As she approached her lover,
hear how she forestalled him: 4
    "S[ir Tristran, by God the King!]
[You do me so great a wrong,]
[sending for me at such an hour!"]
[Then she made a show of weeping.]   8
. . . .
. . . .
. . . .
. . . .   12
. . . .
. . . .
[As. . . . .
["In the name of God, who made the air and the sea,   16
do [not send for me ever again.]
I tell [you, Tristran, once and for all,]
certainly [I should not come].
The king thinks [it is with a sinful love]   20
S[ir Tristran,] that I have loved you].
But [before God I swear my faith]fulness;
may He [send a scourge upon me]
[if anyone but he who had me as a virgin]   24
[ever had my love thereafter a single] day!
[If the wicked men of] this realm,
[in whose place] you once did combat
with the Morholt, when you killed him,   28

lead him to believe, as it seems to me,
that love joins us together –
sir, you have no such inclination;
nor, by Almighty God,   32
do I desire a love affair
that might lead to shame.
I would rather be burned,
my ashes scattered down the wind,   **1b**   36
than, any day of my life, share love
with any man but my lord.
Oh, God! yet he does not believe me!
I can say: how I have been brought down!   40
[S]ir, Solomon said most truly:
[if anyone saves] a thief from the gallows,
[the thief will not love him afterwards, not a single] day.
[If the] wicked men of this realm   44
. . . .
. . . .
. . . .
. . . .   48
. . . they ought to have hidden it from us.
You had to suffer much pain
from the wound you received
in the battle you fought   52
with my uncle. I healed you.
If because of that you were my friend,
it was no wonder, by my faith!
But they have given the king to understand   56
that you love me with a dishonourable love.
Let them see God and His kingdom!
Never would they look Him in the face.
Tristran, take care not to send for me   60
in any place, for any reason;
I should not be so bold
as to dare to come.
I am staying too long here, truth to tell.   64
If the king knew one word about this
I should be torn limb from limb.
I well know that he would have me killed,
and yet it would be quite wrongfully.   68

Tristran, surely the king does not know
that it is for his sake that I have loved you.
Because you were of his kindred   1c
I held you dear.   72
Long ago I believed that my mother
dearly loved my father's relatives;
she used to say that never a wife
would cherish her lord   76
if she would not love his kin.
Indeed, I well know that she was speaking the truth.
Sir, I have loved you much, on his account,
and thereby I have quite lost his favour."   80
"Surely, he [did] not . . . . .
Why would the [. . .] be all his?
His men have made him believe
something about us that is untrue."   84
      "Sir Tristran, what do you mean?
The king, my lord, is very courtly.
Never would he have thought, all by himself,
that we two might be of such a mind.   88
But a man can be misled
into doing wrong and leaving right behind.
So it has been done with my lord.
Tristran, I am leaving, I've stayed here too long."   92
"Lady, for God's love, pity!
I sent for you, and here you are.
Listen a little to my entreaty.
I have cherished you so!"   96
(When he had heard his lover speak
he knew that she had grasped the situation.
He gave praise and thanks to God for it;
now he knew that they would come out of this safely.)   100
"Ah! Iseut, king's daughter,
noble, courtly, loyal,
I have sent for you many times
since entry to your chamber was forbidden me   104
and thereafter I could not speak to you.
Lady, now I wish to cry you mercy   1d
that you may remember this wretch
who lives in affliction and grief.   108

For I am so grieved that the king ever
thought badly of you on my account,
that there is nothing left for me but to die.
My heart is heavy   112
. . . .
. . . .
. . . .
. . . .   116
. . . .
. . . . that he might have been wise enough
not to take a tale-bearer's advice
to send me away from him.   120
The evil, base Cornishmen
now rejoice and joke about it.
Now I see clearly, as I believe,
that they would not want him   124
to have a man of his lineage with him.
His marriage has caused me much harm.
God! Why is the king so foolish?
I would rather let myself be hanged by the neck   128
from a tree, than in all my life
have a love-affair with you.
He does not even let me exculpate myself!
Because of his wicked men he is angry with me.   132
He is very wrong to believe them;
they have deceived him, he sees nothing.
I saw them very still, speechless,
when the Morholt had come here;   136
then there was not a single one of them
who dared take up his arms.
I saw my uncle much perturbed then;
he would rather have been dead than alive.   140
To enhance his honour I armed myself;   **2a**
I fought the Morholt and drove him away.
My dear uncle ought not to have believed
his tale-bearers concerning me.   144
Often I am heart-sick about it.
Does he think that he is not acting wrongly in this?
Yes, wrong will come of it, without fail,
By God, the son of Saint Mary.   148
   Lady, now tell him straightaway

to have a burning pyre made,
and I shall enter it.
If ever I have one hair burned   152
of the hair-shirt I shall have on,
then let him leave me to be quite consumed in the fire,
for I well know that there is no one at his court
who would come forth to do combat with me.   156
Lady, out of your great nobleness,
    has pity for this not seized you?
Lady, I cry you mercy:
Reconcile me with my friend!   160
When I came here to him, from across the sea,
it was as to my liege lord that I meant to turn."
    "By my faith, sir, you do great wrong
in speaking to me of such a matter: 164
that I should address him on your behalf
and make him put aside his anger.
I do not wish to die yet
nor destroy myself utterly.   168
On your account he is highly suspicious of me –
and I am to raise the subject with him?
Then I should be extremely rash.
By my faith, Tristran, I shall not do it   172
and you must not ask it of me.
I am quite alone in this land.
He has forbidden you entry to his chambers
because of me; if now he heard me speak of this   **2b**   176
he might well think me an adulteress.
By my faith, I shall not say a word about it.
And I shall tell you something
and I want you to know it well: 180
if, fair sir, he were to set aside,
for God's sake, his displeasure and anger with you,
I [should be full] of joy.
[But now if he knew of this] visit   184
[I well know that no escape, Tristran,]
[would there be from death.]
[I am leaving, yet shall never sleep.]
[I greatly fear that someone]   188
[may have seen you come here].
[If] the king could hear [one word]

[of our being] together here
he would have me burned on a pyre;   192
it would be no great wonder.
I am shaking, I am very much afraid.
Because of the fear that now seizes me
I am leaving, I have stayed here too long."   196
     Iseut turned away, he called her back.
"Lady, for the sake of God, who in a virgin
took on humanity for humankind,
help me, out of charity!   200
I know that you dare not stay here any longer.
I do not know to whom to turn, if not to you;
that the king hates me I well know.
All my equipment is being held in pledge.   204
Do have it released to me
and I shall flee, I do not dare to remain here.
I know that I have great renown
throughout all the earth where the sun reaches;   208
I know there is no court in the world
where, if I went to it, the lord would not honour me.
And [even] if I ever had anything of his,   2c
Iseut, by this fair head of mine,   212
my uncle would wish not to have thought this
before a year had passed,
for his own weight in gold.
I do not mean to lie to you, even by two words.   216
Iseut, for [God's sake, think of me;]
[acquit me of the debt I owe my host!"]
["By God, Tristran, I am much amazed]
[that you give me such counsel.]   220
[You are seeking my ruin;]
[Such counsel is not loyal.]
[You well know about the suspicion,]
[whether it be based on fact or foolishness.]   224
By God, the glorious Lord,
who formed Heaven and Earth and us,
if he heard a single word spoken
concerning my having you acquitted of your pledges   228
it would be far too much an open matter.
Indeed, I am not so rash.

Nor do I tell you this out of stinginess,
know that for truth!"   232
　　Thereupon Iseut departed;
weeping, Tristran bade her farewell.
Tristran leaned, it seems to me,
on the block of dark marble,   236
lamenting to himself alone.
"Ah, God! Fair lord Saint Evrol!
I did not think to make such a loss
or to flee in such poverty.   240
　　I shall take away neither arms nor horse,
nor any companion except for Governal.
Ah, [God]! A man without equipment –
People make little case of him.   244
When I am in another land
and hear a knight talk of warfare,   **2d**
I shall not dare say a word on the matter;
a man without arms has no right to speak   248
Now I shall have to bear with Fortune,
who has already caused me great harm and rancour.
Dear uncle, [little did he know me,]
[the man who suspected me with regard to your wife.]   252
[I never was inclined to such madness.]
[He would know little of my heart]
. . . .
. . . .   256
. . . .
[The king, who was above in the tree,]
[had clearly seen the meeting]
[and heard the entire conversation.]   260
[For the pity that seized his heart]
[he would not have kept from weeping]
[for any price. He was much grieved;]
[much did he hate the] dwarf of Tintagel.   264
　　["Alas!" said the king,] "now I have seen
[that the dwarf] has greatly deceived me.
He made me climb up [into this tree;]
he [could] not have shamed [me] more.   268
He has caused me to believe a lie
about my nephew; for that I shall have him hanged.

He made me get into a rage
in order to make me hate my wife.   272
I believed him, and was a fool to do so.
The reward for it will be paid:
if I can get my hands on him
I shall put an end to him by fire.   276
Through me he will meet a harsher end
than Constantine inflicted
on Segoçon, whom he gelded
when he found him with his wife."   280
(He had crowned her in Rome;   **3a**
many a worthy man served her;
he cherished and honoured her.
He wronged her, then wept for it.)   284
Tristran had left some time ago.
The king climbed down from the tree.
In his heart he said that he now believed his wife,
and mistrusted the barons of the realm   288
who kept giving him to believe something
that he well [knew not to be] true,
that he had proven to be a lie.
Now he would not [fail to give the] dwarf   292
with his sword what he deserved, so well
that nevermore would he speak slander.
And never again would [Marc] suspect
Tristran on Iseut's account, but would leave   296
the bedchamber to them, just as they wished.
    "Now at last I can be certain.
If the tale were true, this meeting
would not have ended thus.   300
If they loved each other with illicit love,
here they had ample opportunity:
I should indeed have seen them exchanging kisses.
I heard them lament so much!   304
Now I know well that they have no desire for it.
Why did I believe something so outrageous?
It weighs on me and I repent of it.
The one who believes everybody is a great fool.   308
I ought to have established
the truth about those two people,

rather than have a foolish preconception.
It was well for them that they saw this evening come!   312
I have learned so much from their conversation
that never again shall I be uneasy about them.
In the morning Tristran will be reconciled
with me, and he will have leave   **3b**   316
to be in my bedchamber just as he pleases.
Now it is forestalled, that flight
that he intended to make in the morning."
Now hear about the hunchbacked dwarf Frocin!   320
He was outdoors, looking up in the air;
He saw Orion and Venus.
He knew the course of the stars
and would observe the seven planets.   324
[He well knew what was to be.]
[When he would hear a child being born]
he would [count all the events of its life.]
The dwarf [Frocin, full] of cunning,   328
was taking great pains to elude that man
who would separate him from his soul.
   He discerned the conjunction of the stars.
He flushed and swelled up with rage;   332
well he knew that the king greatly threatened him
and would not give up before destroying him.
The dwarf turned quite black and then pale;
very promptly he went fleeing away towards Wales.   336
The king went searching everywhere for the dwarf;
he could not find him, and was much grieved.
Iseut entered her chamber.
Brengain saw that she was pale.   340
She knew that Iseut had heard
something for which her heart was heavy,
she being so changed and colourless.
. . . .   344
She answered: "Dear companion,
I may well be distracted and downcast.
Brengain, I do not want to lie to you:
I don't know who meant to betray us today,   348
but King Marc was up in the tree
where the marble block stands.

I saw his shadow in the fountain.
God made me be the first to speak.   3c   352
About what I had gone there for
never a word was spoken, I assure you,
but prodigious lamenting
and prodigious groaning.   356
I reproached him for repeatedly sending for me,
and he in turn kept begging me
to reconcile him with my lord,
who quite unjustly [was in error]   360
[concerning him, on my account. And I told him]
[that he had requested something very foolish,]
that [I should never come to him again,]
nor [should I speak to the king.]   364
I do not know what [more I may have related;]
There was a great [mass of complaints.]
The king never noticed anything
nor grasped my situation.   368
I got out of the bind."
When Brengain heard this, she greatly rejoiced.
"Iseut, my lady, it is a great mercy
that God, who never lied, has done us   372
when He had you break away
from the interview without going further,
without the king's seeing anything
that might not be taken in good part.   376
God has done a great miracle for you!
He is a true father, and such
that He has no intention to do ill
to those who are good and true."   380
Tristran in his turn had related all to his companion,
how he had conducted himself.
When the companion heard him tell it, he thanked God
that Tristran had done no more there with his beloved.   384
The king could not find his dwarf.
(God! It will be so much the worse for Tristran!)
The king came away to his chamber.   3d
Iseut, who feared him much, saw him.   388
"Sir, in God's name, why are you here?
Are you in pressing need, that you come alone?"

"Queen, it is rather that I come to speak to you
and to ask you something.   392
Do not conceal the truth from me,
for that is what I want to know about the matter."
"Sir, I have never lied to you, [not on any day.]
[If I am] to meet my death [here]   396
I s[hall speak the whole truth of] it;
there will be no [lying, not by one] word."
"L[ady,] have you seen my nephew recently?"
"S[ir, I reveal the] truth to you.   400
You will not believe that I am telling the truth,
but I shall tell it without deceit.
I saw him and then spoke to him;
I was with your nephew under that pine tree.   404
Now kill me for it, King, if you will!
Indeed I saw him. That is too bad,
for you think that I love Tristran
in debauchery and lust   408
I grieve at that so much that I do not care
if you dispatch me to a bad end.
Sir, mercy this once!
I have told you the truth, yet you do not believe me   412
but believe an idle report.
My good faith will protect me.
Tristran, your nephew, came under that pine tree
that is within this garden,   416
and sent for me to go to him.
He said nothing to me, but I owed it to him
to do him at least a little honour;
Through him I am your queen.   420
Indeed were it not for the scoundrels
who tell you what never was,   **4a**
I should gladly show him honour.
Sir, I hold you as my lord;   424
and he is your nephew, I have heard.
For your sake I have loved him so much, sir.
But the wicked ones, the tale-bearers,
who want to have him sent from court,   428
make you believe the lie.
Tristran is going away. May God grant that they

receive vile shame for it!
I spoke to your nephew last night.   432
Like a man in distress he implored,
sir, that I reconcile him with you.
I told him that he should leave,
that never again should he send for me,   436
for I should never again come to him
nor should I speak to you about him.
Sir, you will not believe me:
there was nothing more. If you wish,   440
kill me, but it will be wrongfully done.
Tristran is going away because of the dissension;
I well know that he is passing beyond the sea.
He told me that I should pay for his lodging;   444
I did not want to make any payment on his behalf
nor speak with him at length.
  Sir, now I have told you the truth without fail;
if I lie to you, take my head.   448
Know this, sir, beyond a doubt:
I should have paid his debt
willingly, if had I dared.
Even four small whole gold coins –   452
I would not put even that into his purse
because of your gossiping household.
He goes away a poor man; may God guide him!
You put him to flight through great injustice.   456
He will never go into a country   **4b**
where God is not a true friend to him."
The king knew well that she had spoken truth;
he had heard every word.   460
He embraced her, kissed her a hundred times.
She wept, he told her to be quiet.
Never again would he doubt them a single day
because of an assertion of any tale-bearer.   464
Let them go and come at their pleasure!
The possessions [of Tristran would henceforth be] his,
and his [would be Tristran's.]
Never again [would he believe a Cornish]man.   468
Now [the king told the] queen
[how the wicked dwarf] Frocin

[had] predicted the interview
and how he made him   472
climb well up into the pine tree
to see them at their meeting that evening.
"Sir, were you stationed in the pine tree, then?"
"Yes, lady, by Saint Martin!   476
Never was word said there,
short or long, that I did not hear.
    When I heard Tristran recount
the battle that I had him fight,   480
I felt pity for him; I very nearly
fell down out of the tree.
And when I heard him relate
the suffering that he had to bear at sea,   484
suffering caused by the dragon, of which you healed him,
and the great good you did him,
and when he asked you quittance
of his pledges, I felt such heaviness   488
(you did not wish to acquit him,
nor did one of you approach the other) –
pity seized me, up in the tree.
I smiled to myself, and did nothing more."   **4c**   492
"Sir, to me this is exceedingly welcome.
Now, with certainty, you know
we had plenty of opportunity.
If he loved me with an illicit love   496
you would have seen ample sign of it.
Instead, by my faith, you did not see
that he approached me in the slightest
or embraced me [or kissed me.]   500
This indeed seems certain:
[he did not love me with] a base love.
Sir, [if then you had] not seen us then
surely [you would not have believed us about this."]   504
"By God, [no, indeed!" the king responded.]
"Brengain – [if God give] you honour! – ,
go for my nephew, at his lodgings;
and if he says one thing or another,   508
or does not wish to come on account of you,
say I order him to come to me."

Brengain told him: "Sire, he hates me,
and most wrongly, God knows.   512
He says that through me he has quarrelled with you.
He wishes death upon me, implacably.
I shall go; for your sake he will let it be,
perhaps, and will not touch me.   516
Sire, for God's sake, reconcile me with him
when he comes here!"
(Just listen to what the cunning woman said!
She well acted the part of a good deceiver;   520
she was deliberately playing a game
as she complained of Tristran's ill-will.)
"King, I am going for him," said Brengain.
"Reconcile me with him, and you will do well."   524
The king responded: "I shall make an effort.
Go quickly therefore and bring him here."
Iseut smiled at this, and the king more so.
Brengain went bounding off through the door.   **4d**   528
Tristran was stationed at the wall,
hearing them speak to the king.
He seized Brengain by the arms,
he embraced her, thanked God   532
. . . .
to be with Iseut at will.
Brengain addressed Tristran:
"Sir, here in his house   536
[the king has] spoken much
concerning [you and your] dear beloved.
He has [set aside] his [ill-will] towards you;
now he hates those who oppose you   540
[He has asked me] to come to you;
[I] said that you harbour anger towards me.
Make a great show of [having to be] begged,
of not going there readily.   544
If the king makes a plea on my behalf,
put on a show of ill-humour."
Tristran embraced and kissed her.
He was glad that now he would have his ease again.   548
They went off to the painted chamber
where the king and Iseut were.

Tristran entered the chamber.
"Nephew," said the king, "come forward.   552
Give up your ill-will towards Brengain
and I shall set aside mine towards you."
"Uncle, dear lord, now hear me!
You lightly defend yourself   556
concerning me, you who have placed on me this charge
for which my heart weeps in my body.
I'd have been condemned, and she, disgraced.
Such an outrage, such a felony!   560
We never thought of it, God knows.
Now you well know that he hates you,
the man who makes you believe such a preposterous thing.
Take better advice in future.   **5a**   564
Do not bear anger towards the queen
nor towards me, who am of your kin."
"I shall not, dear nephew, by my faith!"
Tristran was reconciled with the king.   568
   The king gave him leave
to be in the royal chamber. Now he was happy!
Tristran came and went in the chamber;
the king was quite unconcerned about it.   572
Ah, God! Who can be in love
a year or two without revealing it?
For love cannot be hidden;
often one lover made signs to the other,   576
often they came together to talk,
both privately and when people were watching.
They could not expect ease everywhere;
they had to have many a conversation.   580
   At the court there were three barons:
you would never have seen more wicked ones.
They had taken an oath together
that if the king would not   584
make his nephew leave his land,
they would not suffer it any longer;
they would withdraw to their castles
and make war on King Marc.   588
For in a garden under a grafted tree
they had seen, the other day, the fair Iseut

with Tristran in a situation such
as no man ought to tolerate.   592
And several times they had seen them
lying quite naked in Marc's bed.
For when the king went off to the forest
and Tristran said: "Sire, I am going off also,"   596
afterwards he remained behind, entered the chamber;
they were in there together a long while.
"We shall tell him ourselves.   **5b**
Let us go to the king and say to him: 600
whether he may love us or hate us [for it].
we want him to banish his nephew."
They all agreed on this course.
They addressed King Marc,   604
having taken him aside.
"Sire," they said, "things are going badly.
Your nephew and Iseut love each other;
whoever wants to, can know it,   608
and we will not stand for it any longer."
The king heard this, gave a sigh,
bent his head towards the ground.
He did not know what to say, walked back and forth.   612
"King," said the three wicked men,
"by our faith, we shall tolerate it no longer;
for we well know in truth
that you condone their crime   616
and are well aware of this extraordinary thing.
What will you do about it? Now take thought!
If you do not remove your nephew from court
so that he never returns,   620
we shall no longer keep our loyalty to you
nor keep peace with you.
We shall make some of our neighbours leave
the court, for we cannot suffer this.   624
Now we have put this choice to you;
Tell us your whole will."
    "Sirs, you are my vassals.
So help me God, I am much amazed   628
that my nephew has sought my shame;
but he has served me in a strange manner.

Advise me, I charge you.
You must indeed advise me,   632
for I do not wish to lose your service.
You well know, I do not care for pride."   **5c**
"Sire, now send for the sooth-saying dwarf.
Truly, he knows many arts,   636
and so let his advice be taken in this matter.
Send for the dwarf, then let it be settled."
And he came very quickly;
may he be cursed as a hunchback!   640
One of the barons embraced him;
the king declared to him what he had to say.
[Ah! now hear what] treachery
[and what sort of] de[ception]   644
[this dw]arf Frocin spoke to the king!
(May all these sooth-sayers be cursed!
Who ever conceived such wickedness
as did this dwarf, may God curse him?)   648
   "Tell your nephew that he must go to King Arthur
at Carlisle, the walled city,
in the early morning;
let him carry a letter written on parchment   652
to Arthur, at a gallop,
a letter well sealed, closed with wax.
King, Tristran sleeps before your bed.
Before long, this night,   656
I know that he will want to speak to her,
because he will have to go away.
King, go out of the chamber early in the night.
I swear to you by God and the law of Rome,   660
if Tristran loves her illicitly,
he will go to speak with her.
And if he goes to her and I do not know of it,
and if you do not see it, then kill me –   664
you and all your men, every one.
[Those two] will be proven guilty without any oath-taking.
King, now let me see to this
and act as I wish;   668
and keep the errand from him   **5d**
until bed-time."

The king answered: "Friend, it will be done."
They separated; each one went his own way.   672
    The dwarf was of great craftiness;
he committed a very wicked deed.
He went into a baker's shop,
got four deniers' worth of flour,   676
then tied it in a fold of his tunic.
Who ever would have thought of such a trick?
That night, when the king had eaten
and they were bedded down in the hall,   680
Tristran went to attend the king to bed.
"Dear nephew," the king said, "I require of you:
do my bidding, I wish it.
You will have to ride   684
all the way to Carduel, to King Arthur.
Have this letter unfolded before him.
Nephew, greet him in my name;
stay with him only one day."   688
When Tristran had heard about the message
he answered the king about conveying it.
"King, I shall go early in the morning."
"Indeed you will, before the night is over."   692
Tristran was put into great agitation.
Between his bed and the king's
there was a good lance's length.
Tristran formed a very rash plan: 696
he said in his heart that he would speak
to the queen, if he could,
when his uncle had gone to sleep.
God, what a pity! He was too reckless.   700
    At night the dwarf was in the chamber.
Hear how he acted, that night!
Between the two beds he sprinkled the flour   **6a**
so that the foot-prints would be visible   704
if one of them went to the other at night.
(Flour retains the shape of prints.)
Tristran saw the dwarf busy himself
and scatter the flour.   708
He wondered what this meant,
for it was not his custom to act so.

Then he said: "Perhaps
he would be sprinkling flour in that spot   712
so as to see our tracks, if one of us should go to the other.
Anyone who would go now would be acting like a fool.
Later the dwarf would see clearly if I went."
The day before, in the woods, Tristran   716
had been wounded in the leg
by a great boar; he was in much pain.
The wound had bled a good deal;
unfortunately it was not bandaged.   720
Tristran was not sleeping, I am sure;
and the king got up at midnight
and left the chamber.
The hunchbacked dwarf went with him.   724
    Within the chamber there was no light
(no candle or lamp was lit).
Tristran got to his feet.
God! Why did he do it? Listen!   728
He put his feet together, estimated the distance, leapt,
fell from a height onto the king's bed.
His wound burst and bled freely;
the blood issuing from it stained the sheets.   732
The wound was bleeding; he did not feel it
for he was too intent on his delight.
The blood pooled in several places.
The dwarf was outside. By the moon   736
He saw well that they were joined together,
the two lovers. At this he trembled with joy   **6b**
and said to the king: "If you cannot take them
together, go and have me hanged!"   740
    The three wicked men were there,
The ones by whom this act of treachery
was thought out in secret.
The king came back. Tristran heard him,   744
got up from the bed all in a fright,
very quickly leapt back again.
At the leap that Tristran made
the blood dripped – things were going badly –   748
from the wound onto the flour.
Ah, God! What a pity that the queen

had not removed the sheets from the bed!
That night, neither of them would have been proven guilty.   752
If she had taken thought about this,
she might well have defended her honour.
(There was [to be] a great miracle of God,
who protected them, as it pleased Him.)   756
The king came back to his chamber.
The dwarf, who was holding the candle,
came with him. Tristran was making
a show of being asleep,   760
snoring loudly through his nose.
He had remained alone in the chamber
except that at his feet lay
Pirinis, who was not stirring,   764
and the queen lay in her bed.
On the flour the blood appeared, still warm.
The king perceived the blood in the bed;
the white sheets were scarlet with it,   768
and on the flour appeared the trace
of the leap. The king threatened Tristran.
The three barons were in the chamber;
angrily they seized Tristran in his bed.   772
They had taken to hating him   6c
because of his prowess and because of the queen.
They insulted him, threatened him much,
would not fail to see justice done in this matter.   776
They saw his leg bleeding.
"Here is real evidence, all too clear;
you are proven guilty!" said the king.
"Your denial is not worth a pea.   780
Indeed, Tristran, tomorrow, I believe,
you may be certain of being put to death."
He cried out: "Sire, mercy!
For the sake of God, who suffered passion,   784
Sire, may pity for us come over you!"
The wicked men said: "Sire, now avenge yourself!"
"Dear uncle, for myself I care not;
I well know I have come to my end.   788
Were it not for fear of making you angry,
this charge would be dearly bought.

Never, at the risk of their eyes, would they have thought
of ever touching me with their hands.   792
But I have nothing against you.
Now, let it turn to ill or to good,
you will do as you please with *me*
and I am ready to accept it from you.   796
Sire, for God's sake, the queen –
have mercy on *her*!" – Tristran bowed to him –
"for there is no man of your household,
if he spoke this slander   800
that I had formed a love-relationship,
a sinful one, with the queen,
who would not find me armed on the battlefield.
Sire, mercy for her, for God's sake!"   804
The three who were in the chamber
seized Tristran and bound him,
and also bound the queen.
All had turned to very great hatred.   808
(Had Tristran ever known   **6d**
that he would not be allowed to exculpate himself,
he would have let himself be torn apart alive
rather than suffer that he or she be bound.   812
But he had such great trust in God
that he knew and was confident
that if he could come to exculpation,
no one would dare seize   816
or take up arms against him.
He quite expected to defend himself on the battlefield.
Hence he did not wish to behave badly
with regard to the king, through any rash act.   820
For had he known what was afoot
and what was to happen to him and her,
he would have killed all three of them;
the king could never have protected them.   824
Ah, God! Why did he not kill them?
The outcome would have been much better.)
Throughout the city arose the cry
that the two of them had been found together,   828
Tristran and Queen Iseut,
and that the king meant to destroy them.

The great people and the humble were weeping;
one person kept on saying to the other: 832
"Alas! we have so much to weep for!
Ah! Tristran, you are so worthy!
What a pity that through treachery
these scoundrels have captured you!   836
Ah! noble, honoured queen,
In what land will there ever be born
a king's daughter equal to you?
Ah! dwarf, your divining has done this.   840
May he never look God in the face,
the one who finds the dwarf somewhere
and does not strike him in the body with a sword!
Ah! Tristran, such great grief   844
will there be for you, fair, dear friend,   **7a**
when you will so be brought to suffering!
Alas! What grief for your death!
When the Morholt took harbour here,   848
he who was coming for our children,
he so quickly made our barons mute
that there was never a one of them so bold
as to dare arm himself against him.   852
You undertook the fight
for all of us people of Cornwall,
and slew the Morholt.
He wounded you with a javelin,   856
sir; from that you nearly died.
Indeed we should not consent
to your being destroyed here."
The noise and uproar mounted;   860
because of it they all ran straight to the palace.
The king was highly fell and furious;
there was no baron, however strong or bold,
who dared say a word to the king   864
about pardoning Tristran for this misdeed.
Now the day came, the night was past.
The king commanded thorn-bushes to be fetched
and a trench made in the ground.   868
The king, pruning-knife in hand,
ordered vine-stems to be sought out everywhere

and piled up with the thorn-bushes,
hawthorns and blackthorns, with their roots.   872
It was already Prime;
throughout the realm was cried the summons
that all should go to court.
The one who could, rushed there first.   876
The people of Cornwall had gathered together.
Great was the noise and commotion;
there was not one who did not mourn
except for the dwarf of Tintagel.   **7b**   880
   The king told them and showed them
that he meant to have
his nephew and his wife burned in a pyre.
All the people of the realm cried out: 884
"King, you would commit too foul a misdeed
if they were not first put on trial.
Then kill them. Sire, mercy!"
In anger the king responded: 888
"By that Lord who made the world
and all things that are in it,
I should not fail to have them burned in the pyre
at the risk of being disinherited   892
if I am ever called to account for it.
Leave me quite in peace on the matter!"
He commanded the fire to be lit
and his nephew brought;   896
he wanted to burn him first.
They went to fetch him; the king waited.
   Then they led him away by the hands.
(By God, they acted like scoundrels!)   900
Tristran was weeping hard, but it did him no good;
they brought him outside, shamefully.
Iseut wept, she nearly went mad.
"Tristran," she said, "what a pity   904
that you are bound so shamefully!
If I were to be killed, provided you were safe,
it would be a great joy, dear friend;
vengeance for it would still be taken!"   908
   Hear, lords, of our Lord God,
how He is full of mercy;

He does not wish the death of a sinner.
He had received the cry, the weeping   912
that the poor people were making
for those who were in distress.
On the way they were taking   7c
there was a chapel on a hill,   916
situated in the angle of a rock.
It was built overlooking the sea, towards the north.
The part that is called the chancel
was situated on an elevation;   920
beyond, there was nothing but the cliff.
This hill was composed of slaty stone;
if a squirrel were to jump from it
it would die, would never survive.   924
In the apse there was a glass window,
a red one, that a saint had made there.
Tristran addressed his escort:
"Sirs, see, here is a chapel.   928
For God's sake let me enter it!
My life-span is nearly over;
I shall pray God that He have mercy
on me, for I have greatly offended against Him.   932
Sirs, there is only this entry-way;
I see each of you holding his sword.
You well know I cannot get out;
I shall have to come back between you.   936
And when I have prayed to God
I shall return to you in the same way."
    Then one of them said to his companion:
"We can well let him go."   940
They pulled off the bonds; he entered.
Tristran did not move like a sluggard.
Beyond the altar he came to the window,
pulled it to him with his right hand;   944
through the opening he jumped out.
He would rather jump than have his body
burned in the sight of such an assembly.
Lords, there was a great broad stone   948
in the middle of that rocky cliff.
Tristran leapt down onto it very lightly.   7d

His clothes were filled with the wind,
which saved him from falling in a heap.   952
(Cornishmen still call
that stone "Tristran's Leap.")
   The chapel was full of people.
Tristran leapt down. The sand was soft;   956
He sank to his knees in the wet ground.
Those men were awaiting him outside the church,
but in vain; Tristran went off.
(God did him a great mercy!)   960
He fled with long strides along the shore.
He well heard the fire crackling;
he was not minded to turn back,
but ran as fast as he could.   964
   But now hear about Governal!
Sword girded, on horseback,
he had gone out of the town.
He well knew that, if he were overtaken,   968
the king would burn him on his lord's account.
He went fleeing away out of fear.
Tristran's companion showed great love for him
when he did not leave his sword behind   972
but took it up from where it had remained
and was bringing it away with his own.
Tristran caught sight of his companion
and hailed him (having recognized him well).   976
When Governal saw Tristran he was glad
and came up to him with joy.
"Companion, God has had mercy on me;
I have escaped, and now here I am.   980
Alas! wretch, what does it matter?
When I do not have Iseut, it does me no good,
Wretch! that leap I made just now –
Why did I not get killed?   984
Death might come to me too late.   **8a**
I have escaped! Iseut, they are burning you!
Truly, I escaped for nothing.
They are burning her for me; for her I shall die!"   988
   Governal said: "For God's sake, fair lord,
take comfort, do not despair.

Look! here is a dense thicket
all surrounded by a ditch.   992
Sir, let us get into it.
Many people pass by this way;
you will hear much news about Iseut.
And if they burn her, you will   996
never again climb into the saddle
if you do not swiftly take revenge for her.
You will have good help with it.
Never, by Jesus the son of Mary,   1000
shall I lie down in a house
until the three wicked scoundrels
through whom your beloved Iseut is to be destroyed
have met death for it!   1004
If you, fair lord, were killed now
before revenge is taken for her,
I should never have joy, not a single day."
Tristran answered: "May God hear you!   1008
Dear companion, I have not got my sword."
"Yes, you have, for I have brought it."
Tristran said: "Companion, then all is well.
Hereafter I fear nothing except God."   1012
"I also have, under my tunic,
something that will be good and pleasing to you:
a small halberk, strong and light,
which may be useful to you."   1016
"God!" said Tristran. "Give it to me!
By that God in whom I believe,
I would rather be cut into pieces –
if I come to the pyre in time,   8b   1020
before my beloved is cast into it –
if I do not kill those who are holding her."
Governal said: "Do not be hasty!
God may give you something   1024
through which you can much better avenge yourself;
thereby you will not have such trouble
as you might have now.
Now, I see nothing within your power,   1028
for the king is angry with you;
all the townspeople are under orders

and all those of the old city:
by his eyes he has given the general command   1032
that the man who can seize you first
and does not do so, he will have him hanged.
Everyone loves himself more than another;
If the hue and cry were raised against you,   1036
someone might well wish to save you
but would not dare even to think of it."
Tristran wept and grieved deeply.
Indeed, despite all the people of Tintagel,   1040
if someone were to cut him into pieces
so that not one piece held to another,
he would not fail to go there
if his companion did not forbid it.   1044
    Into the chamber ran a messenger
who told Iseut not to weep,
that her friend had escaped.
"God be thanked for it!" she said.   1048
"Now I do not care if they kill me,
or bind me or loose me."
The king had had her so bound,
through his order to the three men,   1052
that they constricted her wrists
to the point where blood was dripping from all her fingers.
"By God!" she said, "if I grieve for myself,   8c
now that the wicked tale-bearers   1056
who were to guard my friend
have lost him (thank God!),
no one should esteem me henceforth.
I well know that the tale-bearing dwarf   1060
and the felons, full of envy,
by whose advice I shall be destroyed,
will still get what they deserve.
May it turn to their destruction!"   1064
    Lords, the news came to the king
that his nephew, whom he was about to burn,
had escaped through the chapel.
He turned black with rage at it;   1068
he did not know how to contain himself for grief.
Angrily he ordered that Iseut should come.

Iseut emerged from the hall;
the noise went up in the street. 1072
When they saw the lady bound –
it was an ugly sight – they were much alarmed.
You should have heard the mourning they made for her,
how they cried to God for mercy! 1076
"Ah! noble, honoured Queen,
what grief they have brought into this land,
those men who have raised this scandal!
Truly, they will be able to put the gain of it 1080
in a very small purse.
May they have heavy damage from it!"
    The queen was led
up to the blazing pyre of thorns. 1084
Dinas, lord of Dinan,
who greatly loved Tristran,
threw himself at the king's feet.
"Sire," he said, "hear me! 1088
I have served you a very long time,
without baseness, faithfully.   8d
You will not in all this realm find a man,
a poor orphan or an old woman, 1092
who because of my position as your seneschal,
which I have held all my life,
gave me one Beauvais penny.
Sire, mercy for the queen! 1096
You want to burn her in the fire
without a trial. This is not right,
for she does not confess to this misdeed.
It will be a grievous thing if you burn her. 1100
    Sire, Tristran has escaped.
Plains, woods, passes, fords –
he knows them well, and he is very fearsome.
You are his uncle, he is your nephew; 1104
To you he would do no harm.
But your barons, if he found them in his power,
would he not ill-treat them?
Your land will yet be laid waste as a result. 1108
Sire, truly, I do not attempt to deny this:
If anyone killed or put into the fire

a single squire on my account,
even if he were king of seven countries,   1112
he would set them at risk from me
rather than that I not avenge it.
Do you think that when so noble a woman is concerned,
one whom he brought from a distant realm,   1116
he would not be grieved if she were killed?
On the contrary, there will yet be great strife over it.
    King, give her to me, as reward
for having served you all my life!"   1120
The three through whom this affair had arisen
had become deaf and dumb,
for they well knew that Tristran was at large;
They greatly feared that he was lying in wait for them.   1124
The king took Dinas by the hand;   **9a**
angrily he swore by Saint Thomas
that he would not fail to pronounce sentence upon her
and have her put into that fire.   1128
Hearing this, Dinas felt much grief.
It weighed on him; never, if he had his wish,
would the queen be killed.
He got to his feet with his head bowed.   1132
"Sire, I am going off to Dinan.
By that Lord who made Adam,
I would never see her burned
for all the gold or wealth   1136
that ever belonged to the richest men
who ever lived since the foundation of Rome."
Then he mounted his war horse and turned away,
head lowered, distressed and sad.   1140
    Iseut was brought to the fire,
quite surrounded by people
who all were howling and crying out,
cursing the traitors to the king.   1144
Tears were streaming down her face.
The lady was dressed in a gown
of dark silk, close-fitting,
finely stitched with fine gold thread.   1148
Her hair reached to her feet;
she had it braided with a golden cord.

Anyone who saw her form and her appearance
would have a very evil heart   1152
if he did not pity her;
her arms were bound very tightly.
There was a leper in Lantyan
by the name of Ivain.   1156
He was amazingly disfigured.
He had come running to see this proceeding;
with him he had a good hundred companions
with their crutches and staves.   9b   1160
You never saw so many as ugly
or as marked with sores or as disfigured.
Each of them was holding his clapper.
Ivain cried to the king in a shrill voice: 1164
"Sire, you want to carry out justice
by burning your wife in this way.
This is severe; but if ever I knew anything
This act of justice will last only a short time;   1168
that great fire will soon have burned her up
and this wind will have scattered the ashes.
That fire will die; in those embers
this justice will soon be over with.   1172
But if you want to take my advice
you will inflict such punishment on her
that she will live, but without honour,
and would rather be dead;   1176
and no one would hear of it
without respecting you the more.
King, would you like to do it in this way?"
The king listened to him, and replied: 1180
"If you show me this, without fail:
how she may live and have no honour –
be sure that I shall be grateful to you;
and if you wish, take some of my wealth.   1184
Never was a manner [of punishment] spoken of,
so painful or so cruel,
but that whoever now might know how
to choose something worse, in the name of God the King,   1188
would not have my love forever."
Ivain answered: "What I am thinking

I shall tell you, quite briefly.
See, I have a hundred companions here.   1192
Give Iseut to us, and she will be our common property.
No lady ever had a worse end.
Sire, there is such great ardour in us   **9c**
that under Heaven there is no lady who, for one day,   1196
could endure intercourse with us.
The clothing sticks to our bodies.
With you she used to be in honour,
in miniver and grey fur, and in pleasure.   1200
She had become acquainted with fine wines there,
in the great upper rooms of dark-grey marble.
If you give her to us lepers,
when she sees our low hovels   1204
and notices our scullery
and has to sleep with us –
Sire, in place of your fine meals
she will have pieces of bread and quarter-loaves   1208
that they send to us at your gates –
by that Lord who dwells above,
when she sees our 'court' –
then she will see discomfort.   1212
Then she would rather die than live;
then Iseut the viper will know well
that she has behaved wickedly;
she would rather be burned in a pyre."   1216
   The king heard him; he remained standing
and for a long while did not move.
He well understood what Ivain had said.
He moved rapidly to Iseut, took her by the hand.   1220
She cried: "Sire, mercy!
Rather than give me to them, burn me here!"
The king gave her to him, and the other man took her.
There were a good hundred sick men   1224
who collected around her.
You should have heard the howling and shouting!
All [the spectators] were seized with pity.
But whoever was grieved at it, Ivain was happy.   1228
Iseut went off, Ivain led her away
straight down to the sandy shore.   **9d**

The mob of the other lepers,
not one of them without his crutch,   1232
went straight towards the ambush
where Tristran was awaiting them.
Governal cried aloud:
"Son, what will you do? Here comes your beloved!"   1236
"God!" said Tristran, "what an amazing thing!
Ah! Iseut, lovely thing,
how you were about to die for me
and I for my part was to perish for you!   1240
Such people, who have their hands on you –
let them be quite sure of this:
if they do not release you straightaway,
such-and-such a one will have cause to regret it."   1244
He whipped the war horse, burst from the thicket,
cried as loudly as he could:
"Ivain, you have taken her far enough.
Let her go quickly, lest with this sword   1248
I make your head fly off!"
Ivain began to take off his cloak;
he cried loudly: "Now to your crutches!
Now it will be clear who is with us!"   1252
If you could have seen those lepers puffing,
taking off their short capes and cloaks!
Each of them shook his crutch at him,
some threatening and others insulting.   1256
Tristran did not want to touch one of them
or strike him on the head or do him any harm.
At the shouting, Governal came up;
he had in his hand a branch of green oak   1260
and he struck Ivain, who was holding Iseut.
His blood fell, flowing to his feet.
Tristran's companion aided him well;
he seized Iseut by the right hand.   1264
(Story-tellers say that they   **10a**
drowned Ivain; they are crude
and do not know the story well;
Beroul has it better in his memory.   1268
Tristran was too noble and courtly
to slay people of such a sort.)

Tristran went off the with queen.
They left the plain; into the woods   1272
went Tristran and Governal.
Iseut rejoiced; now she felt no pain.
They were in the forest of Morrois;
that night they slept on a hill.   1276
Now Tristran was as safe
as if he were in a walled castle.
Tristran was a very fine archer;
he well knew how to handle the bow.   1280
(Governal had taken one
from a forester who owned it,
and had also brought away for him two arrows,
fletched and barbed.)   1284
   Tristran took the bow, went through the wood,
saw a roe-deer, nocked, and shot.
He struck it deeply in its right side.
It cried out, leapt high and fell down.   1288
Tristran took it and came away with it.
He made his shelter: with the sword he was holding
he cut the branches, then made the bower.
Iseut thickly bestrewed it.   1292
Tristran sat down with the queen.
Governal knew about cooking;
with dry wood he made a good fire.
They had much wherewith to play at cooking!   1296
They had neither milk nor salt
at that time in their lodging.
The queen was very weary
because of the fear she had experienced;   **10b**   1300
drowsiness overtook her, she wanted to sleep,
wanted to sleep beside her lover.
   Lords, thus they did for a long time,
deep in the forest.   1304
For a long while they were in this wilderness.
Now hear about the dwarf and how he served the king!
The dwarf knew a private matter about the king,
and no one else knew it. Through a rash act   1308
he revealed it. (He played the fool,
for later the king had his head for it.)

One day when the dwarf was drunk
the barons put to him the question 1312
of what it meant that they conversed so much,
he and the king, and had private speech.
"When it comes to concealing a private matter
the king has always found me very trustworthy. 1316
I see very well that you want to hear it,
yet I do not want to break my faith.
But I shall take the three of you
to the Perilous Ford. 1320
There is a hawthorn there,
with a hollow under its root.
I can stick my head into it
and, outside, you will hear me speak. 1324
What I say will be the secret
about which I am oath-bound to the king."
The barons came to the hawthorn,
the dwarf Frocin coming before them. 1328
The dwarf was short and had a large head;
he had quickly made the hollow [larger].
They pushed him into it up to the shoulders.
"Now listen, lord marquesses! 1332
Hawthorn, I speak to you, not to some nobleman:
King Marc has horse's ears."
They well heard the dwarf speak. **10c**
It happened that one day, after dinner, 1336
King Marc was talking with his barons;
in his hand he was holding a laburnum bow.
Then in came the three
to whom the dwarf had told the secret. 1340
They said to the king in private:
"King, we know what you are concealing."
The king grew angry and said: "This affliction,
that I have horse's ears, 1344
came to me through that soothsayer.
Truly, I shall put an end to him."
He drew his sword and struck off his head.
This was highly pleasing to many people 1348
who hated the dwarf Frocin
for Tristran's sake and the queen's.

    Lords, you have already heard
how Tristran had leapt   1352
all the way down the cliff,
and how Governal, on the war horse,
had come out [of the town], for he feared
that he would be burned, if Marc got hold of him.   1356
Now they were together in the forest.
Tristran fed them with venison.
They were in that wood for a long time;
wherever they took shelter at night   1360
they moved away from it in the morning.
One day, by chance, they came
to Brother Ogrin's hermitage.
They were leading a harsh and wretched life,   1364
yet so much did they love each other with true love
that each because of the other felt no distress.
    The hermit recognized Tristran.
Propped on his staff   1368
he addressed him; hear in what terms:
"Sir Tristran, a great oath   **10d**
had been sworn throughout Cornwall:
whoever turned you over to the king, without fail   1372
would have a hundred marks as reward.
In this land there is no baron
who has not pledged, with his hand in the king's,
to turn you over to him, dead or alive."   1376
Ogrin told him very kindly:
"By my faith! Tristran, whoever repents
through faith and through confession,
to that person God grants pardon."   1380
Tristran said to him: "Sir, by my faith,
if she loves me faithfully,
you do not understand the reason for it.
If she loves me, it is through the potion.   1384
I cannot separate from her
nor she from me; I do not mean to lie about it."
Ogrin said to him: "And what comfort
can one give to a dead man?   1388
He is as good as dead, anyone who long
lies in sin, if he does not repent.

No one can give penance
to an unrepentant sinner."   1392
   The hermit Ogrin sermonized them much
and gave them counsel about repentance.
Again and again he told them
the prophecies of Scripture.   1396
Repeatedly he brought
their separation to their minds.
To Tristran he said, with much urgency,
"What will you do? Take thought!"   1400
"Sir, I love Iseut out of measure,
so much that I do not sleep or slumber.
Once and for all the decision is taken:
I prefer to be a beggar with her   1404
and live on green plants and acorns   **11a**
than have the realm of King Otran.
I do not want to speak about leaving her,
truly, for I cannot do it."   1408
   Iseut wept at the hermit's feet,
changing colour rapidly and often;
repeatedly she cried him mercy:
"Sir, by God Omnipotent,   1412
he does not love me, nor I him,
except through a potion of which I drank,
and he drank of it. That was a pity.
For that the king has driven us away."   1416
The hermit promptly answered:
"Come, come! That God who made the world,
may He give you true repentance!"
And know truly, without a doubt,   1420
they slept that night at the hut of the hermit;
for them he greatly changed his manner of living.
In the morning Tristran left him.
He kept to the woods, left the open fields.   1424
They lacked bread; this was a great hardship.
Stags, hinds, roe-deer –
of these he killed plenty in the woods.
Wherever they took their shelter   1428
they did their cooking and made their good fire.
One night only were they in any one place.

   Lords, hear how on Tristran's account
the king had had his proclamation cried –   1432
in Cornwall there was no parish
where the news of it did not cause dismay –
that whoever might find Tristran
was to raise the hue and cry.   1436
   If someone wants to hear a tale
concerning how important training is,
let him listen to me a little while!
You will hear me speak of a good hunting-dog;   **11b**   1440
no count or king had any such.
He was swift and ever at the ready,
for he was lively, quick, not slow.
His name was Husdent.   1444
He was tethered to a block of wood.
The dog kept looking about in the keep,
for he had been put into great fear
when he did not see his master.   1448
He would not eat bread or mash
or anything anyone gave him.
He kept whining and pawing the ground,
his eyes watering. God! what pity   1452
the dog aroused in many people!
Everyone said: "If he were mine,
I should loose him from the wooden block
for, if he goes mad, it will be a pity.   1456
Ah! Husdent, such a hunting-dog
will never be found again, one so keen
and one that so misses his master.
There never was a beast showing such love.   1460
Solomon spoke judiciously when he said
that his friend was his hunting-dog.
We can prove this by you, Husdent:
You refuse to taste anything   1464
since your master was captured.
King, let him be freed from the clog!"
The king said to himself –
he thought the dog was going mad for his master – 1468
"Truly, the dog has much sense:
I do not believe that in our time

in the land of Cornwall
there is a knight who equals Tristran."   1472
   Three barons of Cornwall
spoke to the king about this matter:
"Sire, untie Husdent!   **11c**
Thus we shall see, for certain,   1476
whether he is grieving so
out of longing for his master;
for no sooner will he be untied
than, if he is mad, he will bite   1480
something, a beast or a person,
and will have his tongue hanging out."
   The king called a squire
to untie Husdent.   1484
They climbed up on benches, on stools,
for at first they feared the dog;
they were all saying: "Husdent is mad!"
None of this interested him.   1488
As soon as he was untied
he ran through the ranks of people, so excited
that he would remain there no longer.
He went out of the hall through the door,   1492
came to the lodging where he used
to find Tristran. The king saw this,
and the others who went after him.
The dog barked and often whined,   1496
showing great distress.
He came upon the trace of his master.
Never had Tristran taken a step
when he was captured and was to be burned   1500
that the dog did not follow,
and each man had to run like a messenger.
Husdent got into the chamber
where Tristran was betrayed and captured;   1504
then he came out, made a leap, went barking
along the cart-track towards the chapel.
The people went after the dog.
After being freed from the tether   1508
he never stopped until he was in the church
situated high above, upon the rock.   **11d**

The lively Husdent, not moving slowly,
entered the chapel through the doorway.   1512
He jumped upon the altar; not seeing his master,
out he went through the window.
He fell down the cliff
and hurt his leg.   1516
He put his nose to the ground and barked.
At the edge of the flowering wood
where Tristran had concealed himself
Husdent paused a little;   1520
then he went on, passing through the wood.
No one saw him who did not pity him.
The knights said to the king:
"Let us leave off following this tracking-dog;   1524
he could lead us into a place
from which it would be difficult to return."
    They left the dog and turned back.
Husdent came upon a cart-track   1528
and was very glad of the path.
The woods resounded with the dog's barking.
Tristran was down in the woods
with the queen and Governal.   1532
They caught the sound; Tristran hearkened to it.
"By my faith," he said, "I hear Husdent!"
They were greatly alarmed.
Tristran jumped up and braced his bow;   1536
They withdrew downhill into a thicket.
They were dismayed, fearing the king;
they said that he was coming with the dog.
Only shortly afterwards   1540
the hunting-dog, following the path,
saw his master and recognized him.
Then he shook his head and wagged his tail.
Anyone who saw him joyfully weeping   1544
might say that he had never seen such joy.   **12a**
He ran to fair-haired Iseut
and then to Governal;
He showed his joy to them all, even the horse.   1548
Tristran felt much pity for the dog.
"Ah, God!" he says, "by what misadventure

has this hunting-dog followed us?
A dog that is not quiet in the woods   1552
is no use to a banished man.
Here we are in the woods, hated by the king;
Lady, in open country, in the woods, through all terrain,
King Marc is having us sought for.   1556
If he found us or could capture us
he would have us burned or hanged.
We have no need of a dog.
Know one thing well: 1560
if Husdent stays with us
he will cause us fear and much grief.
It is better for him to be killed
than for us to be captured because of his barking.   1564
And it grieves me, because of his fine quality,
that here he has sought out death;
    Greatness of nature made him do it.
But how can I avoid the act?   1568
Truly, it greatly distresses me
that I must kill him.
Help me to decide about this;
we need to protect ourselves."   1572
Iseut said to him: "Sir, have pity!
A dog barks when taking its prey,
either by nature or by habit.
Once I heard tell that   1576
before Arthur became king,
a Welsh forester
had a tracking-dog that he had trained in this way:
when he had drawn blood from his stag   **12b**   1580
with the hunting-arrow,
by whatever track the stag fled
the dog would follow by leaps and bounds;
it would not make the woods resound by barking,   1584
nor however much it closed in on its prey
would it give tongue or cause trouble.
Dear Tristran, it would be a great joy
if someone could make the effort   1588
to make Husdent leave off barking
when hunting and closing in on his prey."

Tristran stood still and listened.
Pity seized him. He thought a little,   1592
then said: "If by taking pains
I could put Husdent in the way
of leaving off barking in favour of silence,
I should value him much.   1596
And I shall make the effort
before this week is over.
It would grieve me if I killed him,
and I greatly fear the dog's barking;   1600
for I might be in such a place,
with you or Governal my companion,
where if he barked he would cause us to be captured.
Now I want to take pains and attend   1604
to [making him] take prey silently."
Now Tristran went to hunt in the woods.
He made ready, and shot at a fallow-deer.
Blood flowed, the dog gave tongue,   1608
the wounded deer fled bounding away,
lively Husdent barked loudly,
the woods resounded with his voice.
Tristran struck him, giving him a hard blow.   1612
The dog stopped beside his master,
left off barking, abandoned the prey,   **12c**
and looked up at his master, not knowing what to do.
He dared not bark; he left the trail.   1616
Tristran pushed the dog down;
with a stick he beat the path,
and Husdent tried to bark again.
Thus Tristran began to train him;   1620
before the first month had passed
the dog was so well trained in the wasteland
that he followed his trail without barking.
On snow, on grass or on ice   1624
he would never give up on his prey,
however swift and agile it might be.
   Now the dog was highly useful to them;
he did them good out of measure.   1628
If in the woods he took a roe-buck or a deer
he hid it well, covering it with branches;

and if he caught up with one in open country –
as it happened that he took many such –   1632
he threw much grass over it,
then went back to his master
and led him to where he had taken his prey.
Dogs are very serviceable!   1636
   Lords, Tristran was long in the woods;
there he had many pains and hardships.
He dared not remain in one place;
where he rose in the morning he did not lie that evening.   1640
He well knew that the king was having him sought for
and that it had been proclaimed throughout the land
that whoever might find him was to capture him.
In the wood they were quite deprived of bread;   1644
they lived on meat, eating nothing else.
How could they help turning pale?
Their clothes tore, the branches shredded them.
For a long time they fled through the Morrois.   **12d**   1648
Each of them endured equal suffering,
yet each, because of the other, felt no pain.
The noble Iseut had great fear
lest Tristran might have regrets on her account;   1652
and Tristran in turn was much grieved
that Iseut was in conflict because of him,
[and] might repent of their illicit love.
One of those three (may God curse them!)   1656
through whom they had been exposed –
hear what he did one day!
A powerful man he was, and well-esteemed.
He liked dogs for his pastimes.   1660
(The natives of Cornwall
were so afraid of the Morrois
that not a single one dared to enter it.
They had good reason to fear it: 1664
for if Tristran could capture them
he would make them hang from the trees;
and so they did well to leave it alone.)
One day, with the war horse,   1668
   Governal was alone beside a brook
that ran down from a little spring.

He had taken off the saddle, and the horse
was grazing on the new grass.   1672
   Tristran was lying in his bower;
he was closely embracing
the queen, for whose sake he was
enduring such pain, such distress.   1676
They were both asleep.
Governal was in a secluded place.
By chance he heard dogs;
they were chasing a stag at great speed.   1680
(These dogs belonged to one of the three
by whose counsel the king
was at odds with the queen.)   **13a**
The dogs chased, the stag ran swiftly.   1684
Governal came by a cart-track
onto a heath; far behind (the pack)
he saw coming the man whom he well knew
his lord hated more than anyone else –   1688
quite alone, without a squire.
With his spurs he pricked his war horse
so much that it spurted blood;
he kept striking it on the neck with his stick.   1692
The horse stumbled over a stone.
Governal leaned against a tree;
he was in ambush, waiting for the man
who was coming too fast, and would flee slowly.   1696
   (No one can turn back Fortune.
He was not mindful of the resentment
he had aroused in Tristran.)
The other man, at stand under the tree,   1700
saw him coming and boldly awaited him;
he said to himself that he would rather be cast
to the wind than not take revenge on him,
for through him and his doings   1704
they all had nearly been destroyed.
The dogs followed the fleeing stag,
the baron came after the dogs.
Governal jumped out of his ambush.   1708
Remembering the harm that man had done.
He cut him in pieces with his sword,

took the head, and went off with it.,
The huntsmen, who had started the stag,   1712
were following the dogs as they chased it.
They saw their lord's body,
headless, down under the tree.
Whoever was fastest fled away first.   1716
They believed that Tristran had done this,
the man against whom the king had had the ban proclaimed.   **13b**
Throughout Cornwall they heard
that one of the three had lost his head,   1720
one who had set Tristran at odds with the king.
They all felt fear and anxiety;
since then they left the wood in peace;
little hunting was done there afterwards.   1724
From the moment of entering the wood,
even to hunt, everyone dreaded
that the valiant Tristran might come upon him.
He was feared in the open and more so in the wild wood.   1728
Tristran was lying in the bower,
which was strewn with leaves because of the hot weather.
He was asleep; he did not know
that that man had lost his life,   1732
the one through whom he had nearly got his own death;
he would be glad on learning the truth of it.
    Governal came to the shelter,
holding the dead man's head in his hand.   1736
In the fork of the branch propping up the shelter
he tied it by the hair.
Tristran awoke, saw the head,
leapt to his feet in fright.   1740
His companion cried loudly:
"Don't move, you can feel safe;
I have killed him with this sword.
Know that this man was your enemy."   1744
Tristran was glad of what he heard:
the one whom he most feared had been slain.
    Throughout the country they were all afraid.
The forest was so dreaded   1748
that no one dared to stay in it.
Now [they three] had the woods to themselves.

While they were there in that forest
Tristran invented the Unfailing Bow.   1752
He set it up in such a way, in the woods,   **13c**
that it found nothing it did not kill.
If a stag or deer, going through the woods,
touched those branches   1756
where that bow was set up and drawn,
if it made contact high, it was struck high
and if it made low contact with the bow
it was struck low immediately.   1760
Tristran, with good reason,
gave that name to the bow when he had made it.
It had a very good name, the bow that did not fail
to hit anything it shot at, low or high.   1764
It was of great use to them thereafter;
it enabled them to eat many a large stag.
Game was needful
to sustain them in the forest,   1768
for they had no bread
and dared not go out into the open.
(For a long while they were in exile,
[and the bow] was an amazingly good resource;   1772
they had venison in plenty.)
Lords, it was a summer's day
in the season when the hay is cut,
a little after Pentecost.   1776
   One morning, with dew on the ground,
the birds were singing the coming of the dawn.
From the bower where he had lain
Tristran, sword girded, emerged alone,   1780
and went to look at the Unfailing Bow;
he went through the woods to hunt.
(Before he returned he was in such pain –
did anyone ever have as much pain as they?   1784
But each of them, because of the other, did not feel it;
they had their solace.
Never, since the time when they took to the woods,
did two people drink so much of such a draught.   **13d**   1788
Nor, as related by the story
there where Beroul saw it written,

did any persons love each other so much
or pay for it so dearly.)   1792
   The queen rose to greet him.
The great heat oppressed them heavily.
Tristran embraced her and said:
" . . . ."   1796
"Beloved, where have you been?"
"After a stag, which has wearied me.
I hunted it so long that I ache all over.
Drowsiness has overcome me; I want to sleep."   1800
The bower was made of green branches;
here and there foliage had been added,
and the ground was well strewn.
Iseut lay down first;   1804
Tristran lay down and drew his sword,
placing it between their two bodies.
Iseut had on her shift
(if on that day she had been naked   1808
it would have gone extremely badly for them)
and for his part Tristran had his leggings on.
Upon her finger the queen had
the golden ring from her wedding to the king,   1812
set with emeralds.
The finger had become extremely thin;
the ring was close to falling off.
Hear how they were lying!   1816
under Tristran's neck she had put
her arm; and the other, I believe,
she had thrown over him.
She was embracing him closely,   1820
and he in turn had her entwined in his arms.
Their love was not feigned!
Their mouths were close together,
and yet there was a space   **14a**   1824
so that their bodies were not touching.
No wind was moving, no leaf trembling.
A sun-beam fell on Iseut's face,
which shone more than glass.   1828
Thus the lovers went to sleep,
thinking of no ill whatsoever.

In that spot there were only the two of them,
for Governal, I believe,   1832
had gone off with the war horse
down through the woods to the forester.
   Hear, lords, what a strange thing happened!
It was nearly disastrous for the lovers.   1836
Through the woods came a forester
who had found the trampled places
where they had lain in the woods.
He followed their camp-sites   1840
until he came to the bower
where Tristran had rejoined Iseut.
He saw the sleepers and recognized them well.
His blood ran cold, he was astounded.   1844
He went off with all speed, for he was in fear;
he knew well that, if Tristran awoke,
he himself could offer no other hostage
but that he would leave his head in pledge.   1848
If he fled it is no wonder.
He emerged from the woods, running remarkably fast.
   Tristran slept on with his beloved.
(They were close to meeting their death.)   1852
In the place where they were sleeping,
they were a good two leagues
from where the king was holding his court;
the forester ran at full speed,   1856
for he had heard the proclamation
made concerning Tristran: **14b**
that anyone who would give a truthful report about him
to the king, would receive much of his wealth.   1860
The forester knew this well,
and therefore he ran at such speed.
And King Marc, in his palace
with his barons, was hearing legal actions.   1864
The hall was crowded with barons.
The forester came down the hill
and entered the palace, still moving very fast.
Do you think he ever dared to stop   1868
before he came to the steps
of the hall? Up he went.

The king saw him coming in a great hurry
and hailed him at once: 1872
"Do you know some news, you who come in so fast?
You resemble a man running with dogs,
chasing his prey to catch it.
Do you want to make complaint against someone at court?   1876
You appear to be someone who has a pressing need,
sent here to me from afar.
If you want something, speak your message.
Has anyone denied you his pledge,   1880
or driven you from my forest?"
"Hear me, King, if you please,
Listen to me for a moment.
Throughout this country it has been proclaimed   1884
that if anyone should find your nephew,
he would do better to let himself be killed
than not capture him, or come to make report.
I have found him, yet I fear your anger.   1888
If I point him out to you, will you put me to death?
I shall lead you to where he is sleeping,
and the queen with him.
I saw her with him, a little while ago;   1892
they were fast asleep.   **14c**
I was very frightened when I saw them there."
The king, hearing him, puffed and sighed;
he was troubled, and became very angry.   1896
He said to the forester, speaking
privately in his ear:
"Where are they? Tell me!"
"In a bower in the Morrois;   1900
they are sleeping in close embrace.
Come quickly, we shall be avenged on them.
King, if now you do not take harsh vengeance
you have no right in this land, without a doubt."   1904
The king said to him: "Go outside there.
As you value your life,
say what you know to no one,
whether it be stranger or acquaintance.   1908
At the Red Cross, at the crossroads
where bodies are often buried –

stay there and wait for me.
I shall give you gold and silver,   1912
as much as you wish, I swear it."
The forester left the king,
came to the cross, and sat down.
(May the *gutta serena* blind his eyes,   1916
the one who so wanted to destroy Tristran!
He would have done better to take himself off,
for afterwards he died in such great shame
as you will hear further on in the tale.)   1920
The king entered the chamber;
he summoned to him all his close advisers,
then ordered and enjoined them
not to be so bold   1924
as to go after him one step.   **14d**
Each man said to him: "King, is this a joke,
to go somewhere all by yourself?
There never was a king who did not take precautions.   1928
What news have you heard?
Do not go anywhere on the word of a spy!"
The king answered: "I know of no news,
but a young girl has sent me word   1932
that I should go quickly to speak to her.
She told me not to bring a companion.
I shall go quite alone, on my war horse;
I shall take neither companion nor squire.   1936
This time I shall go without you."
They answered: "This causes us concern.
Cato commanded his son
to avoid solitary places."   1940
He answered: "I know that very well.
Let me do a little as I please."
   The king had his saddle put on,
and girded on his sword. Repeatedly he lamented   1944
to himself the vile act
that Tristran had committed in taking her away,
Iseut the fair with the bright face,
with whom he had fled.   1948
If he found them (he threatened them much)
he would not fail to do them harm.

The king was much minded
to destroy. It was a great pity!   1952
He came forth from the city
saying he would rather be hanged
than not take revenge on those
who had done him such an offence.   1956
He came to the cross, where the other man awaited him,
and told him to go swiftly
and lead him by the direct way.
They entered the wood, which was very shadowy.   **15a**   1960
The spy went ahead of the king,
who had great trust
in the sword that he had girded on
and with which he had struck off many a head.   1964
(Yet here he was acting too much like an overconfident man;
for if Tristran had awakened
and the nephew had become embroiled with the uncle,
one of them would have died before it was all over.)   1968
King Marc said to the forester
that he would give him twenty silver marks if he led him
quickly to the one who had transgressed against him.
The forester (shame upon him!)   1972
said that they were close to their goal.
The spy had the king dismount
from the good war horse, bred in Gascony,
hastening to the off side to hold the stirrup.   1976
He tied the horse's rein
to the branch of a green apple tree.
They had gone only a short distance forward
when they saw the bower they had set out to find.   1980
The king unfastened his cloak
with its clasps of pure gold.
He was lightly clad, his form very handsome.
From its sheath he drew out his sword.   1984
Angrily he moved on, saying repeatedly to himself
that he wanted to die then if he did not kill them.
With naked sword he entered the bower.
The forester went after him,   1988
following the king at a run.
The king gestured to him to turn back.

He raised his sword high;
Anger made him do it, and he broke into a sweat. 1992
The blow was about to fall on them
and kill them (this would have been a great pity!)
when he saw that she was wearing her shift, **15b**
that between them there was a space 1996
and that their mouths were not touching,
and when he saw the naked sword
between the two of them, separating them,
and saw the leggings that Tristran had on, 2000
    "God!" said the king, "What can this mean?
Now I have seen so much of their way of life,
God! I do not know what I should do,
whether to kill or draw back. 2004
They have been here in the woods for a long time.
I can well believe, if I have any sense,
that if they loved each other unlawfully
they would have no clothes on, 2008
there would be no sword between them,
their position would be different.
I had the intention of killing them.
I shall not touch them, I shall put aside my anger. 2012
They have no inclination towards unlawful love.
I shall strike neither of them. They are asleep;
If I were to touch them
I should commit too great a wrong. 2016
And if I awaken this sleeping man
and he kills me or I him,
there will be ugly talk.
I shall make such a sign for them 2020
that as soon as they awaken
they will be able to know, with certainty,
that they were found asleep
and that someone took pity on them. 2024
For I do not at all want to kill them,
neither I nor anyone of my realm.
I see on the queen's finger
the ring with the emerald stone 2028
that I gave to her (it is a very good one);
And in turn I have one that was hers. **15c**

I shall take mine from her finger.
I also have with me a pair of fur gloves   2032
that she brought with her from Ireland.
The sunbeam that burns on her face
and makes her hot – I want to block it with them.
And, when it is time to leave,   2036
I shall take from between the two of them the sword
with which the Morholt's head was cut off."
   The king untied his gloves;
He saw the two sleepers together.   2040
He blocked with the gloves, very gently,
the sunbeam that was falling upon Iseut.
The ring on her finger was within reach;
he drew it off softly so that the finger did not move.   2044
(At first the ring had gone on with difficulty;
but by now her fingers were so thin
that the ring came off without any forcing;
the king was well able to draw it off.)   2048
The sword that was between the two of them
he took away gently, and put his own there.
He emerged from the bower,
came to the horse, and leapt onto its back.   2052
He told the forester to flee,
to take himself off, to be gone.
The king went away, leaving them asleep.
On that occasion he did nothing more.   2056
He returned to his city.
From many sides came questions
as to where he had been and where he had stayed so long.
The king lied to them, he did not reveal   2060
where he had gone or what he had sought
or what he had done.
But now hear about the sleepers
whom the king had left in the woods!   2064
It seemed to the queen   **15d**
that she was in a great forest,
in a rich pavilion.
Towards her were coming two lions   2068
that meant to devour her;
she wanted to cry mercy to them,

but the lions, distressed with hunger,
each was holding her by the hand.   2072
Out of the fright Iseut had from this
she gave a cry and awoke.
The gloves, trimmed with white ermine,
had fallen upon her breast.   2076
    At the cry he heard, Tristran awoke;
his face was quite scarlet.
Alarmed, he jumped to his feet,
seized the sword like an angry man,   2080
looked at it, did not see the notch in the blade.
He saw the golden hilt at the end,
and knew it for the king's sword.
The queen saw on her finger   2084
the ring she had given the king,
saw also that his ring was missing from her finger.
She cried out: "Mercy, sir!
The king has found us here!"   2088
He answered: "Lady, it's true.
Now we must leave the Morrois,
for we have greatly wronged him,
He has my sword, he has left me his;   2092
he might well have killed us."
"Sir, truly, this is my thought."
"Fair one, there is nothing for it but to flee.
He left us only to betray us;   2096
he was alone, and so he has gone for more men.
He expects to capture us, truly.
    Lady, let us flee towards Wales.
My blood runs cold." He turned quite pale.   **16a**   2100
Thereupon their squire arrived,
coming back with the war horse.
He saw that his lord was pale
and asked him what was wrong.   2104
"By my faith, companion, the noble Marc
has found us here asleep.
He left his sword and carried off mine.
I fear that he is plotting treachery.   2108
He has taken the fine ring from Iseut's finger
and has left his own.

By this exchange we can perceive,
companion, that he means to trap us.   2112
For he was alone when he found us.
Fear seized him, and he turned away.
He has gone back for more men,
of whom he has many both bold and fierce.   2116
He will bring them; he wants to destroy
both me and Queen Iseut.
   In the sight of the people he wants to capture us,
have us burned, have the ashes scattered on the wind. 2120
Let us flee, we must not delay!"
They were filled with fear.
(If they were afraid, they could not help it;
they knew the king to be evil-minded and violent.)   2124
They moved away with speed,
fearing the king because of what had happened.
They passed through the Morrois and went on.
Out of fear they travelled far each day;   2128
making straight for Wales.
Love had indeed tried them much;
for three full years they suffered hardship,
their flesh became pale and weak.   2132
   Lords, you have heard of the wine that they drank –
the wine through which they were brought
into such great distress for a long while.   **16b**
But you do not know, I think,   2136
for how long a period the love-drink,
the herbed wine, was intended.
Iseut's mother, who brewed it,
made it for three years of love.   2140
She made it for Marc and for her daughter;
another man tasted of it, and suffered for it.
As long as the three years lasted,
the wine had so overcome Tristran   2144
and the queen along with him
that each of them would say: "I am not weary of it."
   On the morrow of Saint John's Day
the three years were accomplished,   2148
the term for which this wine was intended.
Tristran had risen from his bed;

Iseut remained in her bower.
Know that Tristran   2152
shot a shaft at a stag he had aimed at,
piercing it through the flanks.
The stag fled; Tristran followed it
and pursued it until full evening.   2156
As he ran after the beast
the hour returned, and he stopped –
the hour when he had drunk the love-drink.
Straightaway, alone, he voiced his regret.   2160
"Ah, God!" he said, "how much travail I have!
Today it has been three years, neither more nor less,
that suffering has never failed me,
neither on holidays nor working-days.   2164
I have forgotten chivalry,
forgotten how to follow the court and the noble life.
I am exiled from the land,
am deprived of miniver and grey fur;   2168
I am not at court with knights.
God! My dear uncle would love me so much   **16c**
if I had not done him such wrong!
Ah, God! How badly it goes for me!   2172
    Now I ought to be at a royal court
and a hundred young noblemen with me
who would serve to win their arms
and give me their service.   2176
I ought to go into another land
to offer my own service and seek rewards.
And I am distressed on account of the queen,
to whom I give a bower in lieu of a tapestried chamber.   2180
She is in the woods, and she might be
in fine chambers, with her suite,
chambers hung with silken draperies.
For me she has taken a bad road.   2184
To God, who is Lord of the world,
I cry mercy, that He might give me
the inclination to leave
to my uncle his wife, and in peace.   2188
    I swear to God that I should do it
most willingly, if I could do so

in such a way that Iseut might be reconciled
with King Marc, to whom she was wedded,   2192
alas, in the sight of many a noble man,
in accordance with what is called the Rite of Rome."
    Tristran leaned on his bow,
expressing over and over his remorse about King Marc,   2196
his uncle, to whom he had done such wrong
and put his wife so much at odds with him.
Tristran was lamenting, that evening.
Hear how it was with Iseut!   2200
She kept saying: "Alas! Wretched woman!
Why did you have the gift of youth?
You are in the woods just like any serving-woman;
you find few to serve you here.   2204
I am a queen; but I have lost the name   **16d**
of queen through my potion
that we drank at sea.
Brengain did this, she who was to see to it.   2208
Alas! She kept such poor oversight!
(She could not be blamed, if she acted very wrongly.)
The damsels of the fiefs,
the daughters of the noble vavasors –   2212
these I ought to have about me
in my chambers, to serve me,
and I ought to arrange marriages for them
and give them to husbands for their advantage.   2216
    Dear Tristran, far astray
she sent us, the one who
brought us the love-potion to drink together;
she could not have betrayed us more completely."   2220
Tristran said to her: "Noble Queen,
we are spending our youth in a bad way.
Fair friend, if I could manage,
through counsel that I might obtain about it,   2224
to make a reconciliation with King Marc
so that he would set aside his anger
and would take our formal assurance
that never, not one day, neither in act nor in word,   2228
have I had a love-relationship with you
that would make for his shame –

there is no knight in his kingdom,
nor from Lidan as far as to Durham,   2232
who, if he wanted to say that
I had shared a dishonourable love with you,
would not find me on the battlefield, in arms.
And if it was the king's wish,   2236
when I had cleared you of the charge,
that he would suffer me to be of his household,
I should serve him with great honour
as my uncle and my lord.   **17a**   2240
He would have in his land no man serving at arms
who would better support him in his war.
And if it were his pleasure
to take you back and to dismiss me   2244
(since he might not care for my service),
I should go off to the King of Dumfries,
or cross over to Brittany
with Governal and no other companion.   2248
    "Noble Queen, wherever I may be,
I should always call myself yours.
I should not seek this separation
if our being together were possible,   2252
and if it were not, fair one, for the great deprivation
that you endure and have endured
every day, for me, in the wilderness.
For me you have lost the name of queen.   2256
You might be in honour
in your chambers, with your lord,
were it not, lady, for the herbed wine
that was given us on the sea.   2260
Iseut, noble, fair of form,
counsel me as to what we shall do."
"Sir, Jesus be thanked
that you want to abandon sin!   2264
My friend, remember the hermit
Ogrin, who preached to us from the Written Law
and told us so much
when we turned in at his dwelling,   2268
at the edge of this wood.
Dear sweet friend, if the inclination

to repent has now come upon you,
it could indeed not come at a better time.   2272
Sir, let us hasten back to him!
I am quite confident:
that he would give us honourable counsel   **17b**
through which we may yet   2276
come to eternal joy."
Tristran heard her, gave a sigh,
and said: "Queen of high birth,
let us turn back to the hermitage!   2280
This very night, or in the morning,
with the counsel of Master Ogrin
let us inform the king of our intention
through a letter, without any other message."   2284
"Dear Tristran, you say very well.
To the powerful Heavenly King
we may both cry
that He may have mercy on us, Tristran, my love!"   2288
They turned back in the forest.
The lovers walked until
they came together to the hermitage.
They found the hermit Ogrin reading.   2292
When he saw them he hailed them amiably.
They sat down in the chapel.
"Exiles, to what great distress
love drives you by force!   2296
How long will your folly last?
You have led this life for too long.
Come now! Do repent!"
Tristran said to him: "Now listen!   2300
If we have led it for a long while,
such was our destiny.
For a good three years, neither more nor less,
travail has never left us.   2304
If now we could find counsel
about reconciling the queen with her husband,
never again, not one day, shall I seek
to be with King Marc as my lord,   2308
but shall go off before a month passes
to Brittany or to Loenois.   **17c**

And if my uncle wants to suffer me
to be at his court to serve him,   2312
I shall serve him as I am obliged to do.
Sir, my uncle is a powerful king.
. . . .
Give us your best counsel,   2316
for God's sake, sir, concerning what you are hearing,
and we shall do your will."
   Lords, now hear about the queen!
She fell down at the hermit's feet,   2320
and was not half-hearted in imploring him
to reconcile them with the king:
"For I shall have no inclination towards illicit love
on any day of my life.   2324
I do not say (for your understanding)
that I feel remorse for a single day about Tristran,
or that I do not love him with good love
and as a friend, without dishonour.   2328
As for the carnal union of my body
and his, we are entirely free of it."
The hermit heard her speak, and wept;
he praised God for what he had heard.   2332
"Ah, God! fair, omnipotent King,
with my whole heart I give You thanks,
You who have let me live
until these two people have come   2336
to me to obtain counsel about their sins.
I may well give You great thanks for it.
I swear by my faith and my religion
that you two will have good counsel from me.   2340
Tristran, hear me a little,
you who have come here to my dwelling,
and you, queen, hearken
to my words, do not be foolish.   2344
   "When a man and a woman commit sin,
if they have first taken each other, and then have separated   **17d**
and have come to acknowledge their fault
and have true repentance,   2348
God pardons them for their transgression,
however horrible and ugly it might be.

Tristran, queen, now listen
a little and pay attention to me.   2352
In order to take away shame and cover up evil
it is needful to lie a little, fittingly.
Since you have asked counsel of me
I shall give it to you straightaway.   2356
I shall make a letter out of parchment.
There will be greetings at the top.
Send it to Lantyan.
To the king, with good-will, send greetings.   2360
Say you are in the woods with the queen;
but if he wanted to take possession of her
and would put aside his anger,
you would do this much for him: 2364
you would go to his court.
If then there should be anyone there, wise or foolish,
who wanted to say that you had
formed a base love-relationship,   2368
may King Marc have you hanged
if you cannot defend yourself!
    "Tristran, I dare to advise you so for this reason:
you will never find at court your equal   2372
who will give a pledge to fight against you.
I give you this counsel in good faith,
for the king cannot deny this:
when he wanted to deliver you to death   2376
and burn you in a fire because of the dwarf –
both courtly people and commoners saw it –
he refused to hear a plea.
When God had shown you such mercy   2380
that you had escaped from there,   **18a**
as has been widely heard –
for had it not been for God's power
you would have been destroyed in dishonour   2384
(you made such a leap that there is no man
from Constantine to Rome
who would not shudder if he had seen it) –
from there you fled, out of fear.   2388
You rescued the queen,
and since then have been in the forest.

You brought her from her own land,
gave her to him in marriage –   2392
all this was done, he well knows –
she was wedded in Lantyan.
It would have been wrong of you to fail her;
with her you preferred to flee.   2396
If he wants to hear your defence
so that the high and the low will see it,
you offer to present it at his court.
And if seems to him   2400
that you are loyal to him,
on the advice of his vassals
let him take back his noble wife.
And, if you know that this does not displease him,   2404
you will be with him as his man-at-arms;
you will serve him very willingly.
And if he does not want your service,
you will cross the sea of Dumfries   2408
and go to serve another king.
Such will be the message." "And I agree.
Let this much more, Brother Ogrin,
by your leave, be put on the parchment: 2412
that I dare not be unwary;
he has had a proclamation cried against me.
But I beg of him, as of a lord
whom I greatly love in true love,   **18b**   2416
that he in turn have another letter made
and that in it he have written whatever pleases him.
At the Red Cross, out on the heath,
let his letter be hung, so let him command it.   2420
I do not dare to let him know where I am;
I fear he may do me harm.
I shall indeed trust him when I have
the letter; I shall do whatever he wishes.   2424
Master, let my letter be sealed;
On the tag you will write: 'Vale!'
For the moment I know of nothing more [to say]."
Ogrin the hermit got up,   2428
took pen and ink and parchment,
and set down all these words.

When he had done he took a ring
and impressed the stone on the wax.   2432
Once the letter was sealed, he handed it to Tristran,
who received it very willingly.
"Who will carry it?" said the hermit.
"I shall." "Tristran, do not say that!"   2436
"Truly, sir, indeed I shall do it;
I am well acquainted with Lantyan.
Ogrin, good sir, by your leave,
the queen will remain here.   2440
And soon, in the dusk,
when the king is sleeping soundly,
I shall mount my war horse,
taking my squire with me.   2444
Outside the town there is a slope;
there I shall dismount, and go forward.
My companion will watch my horse;
neither layman nor priest ever saw a better one."   2448
    That evening, after sunset,
when the sky began to darken,
Tristran went off with his companion.   **18c**
He was familiar with the lie of that whole country.   2452
They travelled until they reached
the city of Lantyan.
He dismounted and entered the town.
The watchmen were sounding their horns loudly.   2456
He slipped down into the moat
and went rapidly up to the hall.
(Tristran put himself into much danger.)
He came to the window where the king was sleeping,   2460
and softly called to him
(he did not care to cry halloo).
The king awakened, and promptly said:
"Who are you, who are going about at such an hour?   2464
Have you some pressing need? Tell me your name!"
"Sire, they call me Tristran.
I bring a letter, and I am putting it down here
on the window-sill of this chamber.   2468
I dare not speak to you for long;
I am leaving the letter; I do not dare to stay."

   Tristran turned away. The king jumped up
and called to him aloud three times: 2472
"For God's sake, dear nephew, wait for your uncle!"
The king took the letter in his hand.
Tristran remained there no longer;
He lost no time in taking himself off.   2476
Coming to his waiting companion,
he leapt lightly onto his war horse.
Governal said: "Fool, do hurry!
Let's get away by the side roads!"   2480
They travelled through the woods
until at daybreak they came [back] to the hermitage.
In they went. Ogrin was praying
as fervently as he could to the Heavenly King   2484
that He protect from harm both Tristran
and Governal, his squire.   **18d**
When he saw them, how happy he was!
He thanked his Creator.   2488
As for Iseut, there is no need to ask
whether she had been fearful about meeting them [ever again].
Never since the evening, when they had left the place,
until she and the hermit saw them [once more]   2492
had her eyes been dry of tears;
this space of time had seemed to her very long.
When she saw them come, she asked …
(she was no fool) what he had done there: 2496
"Friend, tell me – so may God grant you honour!
were you at the king's court, then?"
Tristran told them everything:
how he had been to the town   2500
and spoken with the king,
how the king had called him back;
and he told about the letter he had left
and how the king had found it.   2504
  "God!" said Ogrin, "I give Thee thanks!
Tristran, be sure that very soon
you will hear news of King Marc."
Tristran dismounted and put down his bow.   2508
Now they stayed at the hermitage.
The king had his baronage awakened.

[But] first he sent for his chaplain
and gave him the letter he had in his hand.   2512
The chaplain broke the wax and read the letter.
At the top he picked out [the name of] the king,
to whom Tristran was sending greetings.
He quickly grasped all the words   2516
and read the message aloud to the king,
who listened to it willingly.
He rejoiced greatly,
for he deeply loved his wife.   2520
    The king had his barons awakened,   **19a**
sending for the most valued ones by name.
And when they had all come
and fallen silent, the king spoke: 2524
"Lords, a letter has been sent to me here.
I am your king, you are my marquesses.
Let the letter be read and heard;
and when the writing has been read aloud,   2528
counsel me about it, I charge you.
It is your duty to give me good counsel on this."
    Dinas stood up first,
and said to his peers: "Lords, hearken!   2532
If now you hear that I do not speak well,
do not believe me about a single thing.
He who can speak better, let him speak!
Let him do what is right, and leave folly behind!   2536
The letter is sent here to us
from we know not where.
Let the letter be read first of all
and then, according to the message,   2540
whoever knows how to give good counsel,
let him give it to us! I will be plain about this:
whoever gives bad advice to his rightful lord
cannot commit a more unseemly act."   2544
The men of Cornwall said to the king:
"Dinas has spoken like a most courtly man.
Master chaplain, read the letter
in the hearing of us all, from beginning to end."   2548
At that the chaplain rose,
unfolded the letter with both hands,

and remained on his feet before the king.
"Now listen, hear me! 2552
Tristran, our lord's nephew,
first sends greetings and love
to the king and all his baronage.
[Then] 'King, you well know [how] the marriage **19b** 2556
of the King of Ireland's daughter [came about].
On that account I went by sea as far as that land
and won her through my prowess,
killing the great crested dragon. 2560
For this deed she was given to me.
I brought her into your country.
King, you took her to wife
in the sight of your knights. 2564
You had been with her only a short time
when tale-bearers in your realm
brought you to believe a lie.
I am quite ready to engage myself, 2568
if anyone should want to bring an accusation against her,
to exculpate her against any peer of mine,
fair Sire, on foot or on horseback –
let each man have arms and a horse – 2572
to prove that she never had love for me
or I for her, in any unlawful way.
If I cannot exculpate her of this charge
and clear myself in your court, 2576
have me burned before your army.
There is no baron of yours whom I exempt from this;
There is no baron who, to bring me down,
would not have me burned or torn apart. 2580
You well know, fair uncle, Sire,
that in anger you wanted to burn us;
but God was seized with great pity for us,
and for it we praise the Lord God. 2584
It happened that the queen
escaped this fate. This was right,
so God save me! for very wrongfully
you wanted to put her to death. 2588
(I [also] escaped from this, and made a leap
down a very high rock.) **19c**

Then the queen was given
to the sick men for punishment.   2592
I carried her off from them, took her from [their leader];
afterwards I have always been in flight with her.
I could not fail her
given that she nearly died, wrongfully, for me.   2596
Since then I have been with her in the woods,
for I was not so bold
as to dare show myself in the open.
. . . .   2600
to capture us and deliver us to you.
You would have had us burned or hanged,
therefore we had to flee.
But if now it were your pleasure   2604
to take back Iseut with the bright face,
there would be no baron in this land
who would serve you better than I.
If someone sets you on another course   2608
so that you do not want my service,
I shall go off to the King of Dumfries.
I shall pass beyond the sea;
you will never hear of me again.   2612
   'Take thought about what you are hearing, king!
I can no longer suffer such torment.
Either I shall be reconciled with you
or I shall take away the king's daughter   2616
to Ireland, where I got her.
She will be queen of her own country.'"
The chaplain said to the king:
"Sire, there is no more in this writing."   2620
   The barons had heard the request,
that for the King of Ireland's daughter
Tristran was offering to do battle against them.
There was not a baron of Cornwall   2624
who did not say: "King, take back your wife!
Never did they have any sense,   **19d**
those who say this concerning the queen,
who is being talked about here.   2628
I cannot advise you
that Tristran should remain on this side of the sea.

Let him go to the powerful king in Galloway,
on whom the Scottish king is waging war.   2632
It may be that he will so conduct himself there,
and you may hear so much about him,
that you will send him word to come back.
We do not know where else he might go.   2636
Send him word by letter
that he is to bring the queen here, with little delay."
The king hailed his chaplain:
"Let this letter be made with a speedy hand!   2640
You have heard what you are to put in it.
Hurry with the letter! I am much troubled;
it is a very long time since I saw the noble Iseut.
She has borne much distress in her youth!   2644
And when the letter is sealed,
hang it on the Red Cross.
Let it be hung there this very night!
Write on it greetings in my name."   2648
When the chaplain had written it
he hung it on the Red Cross.
    Tristran did not sleep that night.
Before midnight came   2652
he had traversed the White Heath
carrying the sealed letter.
(He was well acquainted with Cornwall.)
He came to Ogrin and gave it to him.   2656
The hermit took the document,
read the characters, saw the nobleness
of the king, who was setting aside
his anger against Iseut, and [read]   **20a**   2660
what he wished: to take her back so graciously.
He saw the date of the reconciliation.
He would indeed speak as he should
and like a man who believes in God: 2664
    "Tristran, what joy is coming to you!
Your message received a swift hearing,
for the king is taking back his wife.
All his people have so advised him.   2668
But they dare not advise him
to retain you as a fighter in his service.

But go to another land for a year or two,
to serve a king on whom war is being waged.   2672
If [then] the king so wishes,
return to him and to Iseut.
On the third day from now, with no deception,
the king is ready to receive her.   2676
The proceeding between them and [the two of] you.
is to take place before the Perilous Ford.
There you will return her to him; there she will be taken back.
This letter says nothing more."   2680
    "God!" said Tristran, "what a separation!
Wretched is the man who loses his beloved.
It must be done, because of the distress
you have endured on account of me.   2684
You have no need to suffer any more.
When it comes to the time of separation,
I shall give you my pledge of love,
and you yours to me, fair beloved.   2688
Never shall I be in any land
where either peace or war may keep me
from sending word to you.
Fair beloved, convey to me in turn   2692
whatever you please, entirely!"
Iseut spoke with a great sigh:
    "Tristran, listen a moment: **20b**
leave me Husdent, your hunting-dog.   2696
Never was a hunter's dog
kept in such honour
as this one will be, my dear friend.
When I see him, it seems to me,   2700
I shall often remember you.
I shall never have so heavy a heart
that, seeing him, I shall not be happy.
Never, since the Law was proclaimed,   2704
was a hunting-dog so well housed
or given so rich a bed.
    Dear Tristran, I have a ring;
a green jasper forms the seal   2708
Fair sir, for love of me
wear the ring on your finger;

and if it comes, sir, into your mind
to send me anything by a messenger 2712
(I shall tell you this much, and know it well),
truly, I should not believe a word of it
if, sir, I did not see this ring.
But, for no king's prohibition, 2716
if I see the ring, I shall not fail,
whether it be wisdom or folly,
to do what he says,
he who brings me this ring, 2720
provided that it be to our honour.
I promise you this in the name of true love.
Beloved, will you give me such a gift as this:
the lively Husdent, on the leash?" 2724
And he answered: "My own beloved,
I give you Husdent as a love-token."
"Sir, I thank you.
Since you have given me possession of the dog, 2728
take the ring in exchange."
She took it from her finger and put it on his.   20c
For this Tristran kissed the queen
and she him, as [a sign of] taking possession. 2732
    The hermit went off to the Mount
because of the rich things that were there.
He promptly purchased furs grey and white,
cloths of silk and dark purple, 2736
dyed woollen cloths, and white linens
far whiter than the lily,
and a smoothly ambling palfrey
well harnessed with shining gold. 2740
Ogrin the hermit bought so much,
and obtained on credit and bartered so much
for precious cloth, grey and white fur, and ermine,
that he dressed the queen richly. 2744
Throughout Cornwall the king had his agreement
with his wife proclaimed:
"In front of the Perilous Ford
our reconciliation will be made." 2748
The report of this was heard everywhere.
No knight or lady remained at home,

none who did not come to this assembly.
They had greatly longed for the queen;   2752
she was loved by all –
except for the wicked men, may God destroy them!
(This is the compensation all four of them got for it:
two died by the sword,   2756
the third was killed by an arrow;
in pain they died in the land.
The forester who denounced [the lovers]
did not avoid a cruel death for it,   2760
for Perinis, noble and fair-haired,
later killed him in the woods with a club.
God avenged them on all these four,
He who willed to bring down their fierce pride.)   2764
   Lords, on the day of the meeting   **20d**
King Marc was with a very large crowd.
There, they had set up many a pavilion
and many a baron's tent;   2768
they had occupied the meadow well into the distance.
Tristran rode with his beloved.
he rode and saw the boundary stone.
Under his tunic he had his halberk on,   2772
for he was greatly fearful on his own account
because he had wronged the king.
He caught sight of the tents in the meadow,
recognized the king and the assembly.   2776
He addressed Iseut gently:
"Lady, you are keeping Husdent.
I pray you, for God's sake, to care for him.
If ever you loved me, then love him.   2780
There is the king, your lord,
with him the men of his realm.
We cannot much longer
go speaking together, the two of us.   2784
I see those knights coming,
and the king and his men-at-arms,
Lady, who are coming towards us.
In the name of God, the powerful and glorious,   2788
if I send you [word about] anything,
whether soon or after a long time,

Lady, do as I ask!"
"Dear Tristran, now listen to me!   2792
By the faith that I owe you,
if you do not send me that ring from your finger
so that I see it,
I shall believe nothing [a messenger] might say.   2796
But as soon as I see the ring again,
neither tower nor wall nor stronghold
will keep me from doing immediately
my lover's bidding,   21a   2800
according to my honour and loyalty
and provided I know it is your will."
"Lady," he said, "God reward you!"
He drew her to him, folded her in his arms.   2804
Iseut, who was no fool, said:
"Beloved, attend to my words!
It is well to listen to me now.
You are escorting me, and mean to give me back   2808
to the king, by the counsel of Ogrin
the hermit (may he have a good end!).
In God's name I beg you, very dear friend,
not to depart from this country   2812
   until you know how the king
will behave towards me – angry or suspicious.
I beg this of you, I who am your dear beloved:
that when the king has taken me back   2816
you go to the home of Orri the forester
at night, to take shelter.
Do not mind staying [there] for my sake.
We lay there many a night   2820
in our bed that I caused to be made for us.
The three who were of evil origin
will meet evil in the end.
May their bodies lie supine in the woods,   2824
my dear friend, and (as I expect it will),
may Hell open and swallow them!
I expect this, for they are very wicked.
You will have entered that fine cellar,   2828
under the hut, my own friend.
I shall send you, by Perinis,

the news of the king's court.
My own friend – may God grant you honour! –   2832
I shall send you word, from here, of my situation (ms. 2835)
by my valet, to you and your companion. (ms. 2836)
You will often see my messenger. (ms. 2834)   **21b**
May staying there not displease you!" (ms. 2833)   2836
"No more it will, my dear love.
He who accuses you of lewd conduct,
let him beware of me as of an enemy!"
"Sir," said Iseut, "great thanks!   2840
Now I am very fortunate;
you have brought me to a fine conclusion."
    They went on so far and the others approached
until they exchanged greetings.   2844
The king was coming, very haughtily,
a bow-shot in front of his men;
with him [was] Dinas, of Dinan.
By the rein Tristran was holding   2848
the queen, whom he was escorting.
There he greeted [him] as he ought:
"King, I restore to you the noble Iseut.
Never did a man make so rich a restitution.   2852
I see here the men of your land,
and in their hearing I wish to require of you
that you permit me to justify myself
and to prove in your court   2856
that never did I have illicit love for her,
nor she for me, not a single day of my life.
You have been made to believe a lie;
but – so God give me joy and well-being! –   2860
they never brought this to judgment.
To fight on foot or otherwise,
within your court – Sire, permit me this.
If I am proven guilty, then burn me in sulphur.   2864
And if I can come out of it safely,
let there be be no man, with hair or bald …
and so retain me with you,
or I shall go off to Loenois."   2868
    The king spoke with his nephew.
Andret, born at Lincoln,   **21c**

said to him: "King, do retain him;
you will be the more respected and feared for it."   2872
He was very close to granting this;
his heart greatly softened.
The king drew him aside;
leaving the queen with Dinas,   2876
who was very true and loyal
and accustomed to acting honourably.
He sported and joked with the queen;
from her neck he removed the cloak,   2880
which was of a very rich dyed material.
She had on a tunic
[and] over it, a wide silken gown.
What should I tell you about her cloak?   2884
The hermit who bought it
never regretted the high price.
The clothing was rich and the body noble;
she had clear eyes and golden hair.   2888
The seneschal was having a pleasant time with her.
This much displeased the three barons.
(May they have ill fortune! They were malevolent.)
Now they drew nearer to the king.   2892
"Sire," they said, "listen to us;
we shall give you counsel, meaning well.
The queen has been accused,
and she fled from your country.   2896
If they are together again at your court
people will surely say, it seems to us,
that their wickedness is being condoned.
There will be few who do not say so.   2900
Let Tristran leave your court;
and after a year has passed
and you are assured
that Iseut is keeping faith with you,   2904
send word to Tristran to come to you.   **21d**
This we advise you, in good faith."
The king responded: "Whatever anyone may say,
I shall not swerve from your advice."   2908
The barons came back;
in the king's name they announced his decision.

When Tristran heard there was to be no delay,
that the king willed his departure,   2912
he took leave of the queen.
They looked at each other lovingly.
The queen was flushed;
she was embarrassed because of the crowd.   2916
Tristran turned away from her. I believe,
God! he made sombre many a heart that day.
The king asked where he would go.
Whatever he wished, he would give it all to him.   2920
He put at his complete disposal
gold and silver, and furs grey and white.
Tristran said: "King of Cornwall,
I shall not take one pennyworth of it.   2924
With what resources I have, I am going to Galloway,
to the rich king on whom war is being waged."
   Tristran had a very rich escort
of the barons and of Marc the king.   2928
Tristran made his way towards the sea.
Iseut escorted him with her eyes;
as long as she had sight of him
she did not stir from the spot.   2932
Tristran went off; those who had accompanied
him for a time returned.
Dinas was still escorting him;
He kissed him over and over, and kept entreating him   2936
to return to him without fail.
The two of them pledged faith to each other.
"Dinas, hearken to me a little!
I am leaving here, you well know why.   **22a**   2940
If I send you word by Governal
of anything urgent,
see to it as you should!"
They kissed each other seven times and more.   2944
Dinas begged him never to fear on his account;
let him speak his wish, [Dinas] would carry it out entirely.
The leave-taking of these two was very fine …
But, on his pledged faith,   2948
[Dinas] would keep her with him
(he would surely not do so for the king).

Thereupon Tristran turned away from him;
at their separation they both were downcast. 2952
  Dinas came back to the king,
who was awaiting him on a heath.
Now the barons rode
towards the city at full speed. 2956
The whole population came out of the town;
there were more than four thousand,
men, women, and children …
Both for Iseut and for Tristran 2960
they were showing extraordinary joy;
the bells were ringing throughout the city.
(When they heard that Tristran was departing,
not a single one did not show deep grief.) 2964
They were rejoicing greatly for Iseut
and were going to much trouble to serve her;
this is why (you are to know), there was no street
that was not draped with silken cloths; 2968
whoever did not have silk put out a bed-curtain.
Along the route the queen followed,
the street was very well bestrewn.
Uphill, along the paved road, 2972
they made for the church of Saint Samson:
The queen and the barons
went all together. **22b**
Bishop, clerks, monks, and abbots 2976
all came out towards her,
dressed in albs and copes.
And the queen dismounted;
she was dressed in a precious dark-blue fabric 2980
The bishop took her by the hand
and brought her into the church.
They led her straight to the altar.
The valiant Dinas, to whom this task was most pleasing, 2984
brought her an adornment
that was worth a good hundred marks of silver:
a rich silken cloth made with gold thread;
never did earl or king have anything like it. 2988
And Queen Iseut took it
and, out of a good heart, put it on the altar.

(From it was made a chasuble,
which was never taken from the treasury   2992
except on the great annual feast days.
It is still at Saint Samson's;
so say those who have seen it.)
Thereupon she emerged from the church.   2996
The king, the princes, and the counts
led her away to the lofty palace.
There they made great rejoicing, that day.
Never was a door forbidden there;   3000
whoever wanted to enter could eat;
refusal was made to no one.
All honoured her much, that day.
Not even on the day she was married   3004
did anyone do her such great honour
as was done her on that day.
That day, the king freed a hundred serfs
and gave arms and halberks   3008
to twenty squires, whom he knighted.
Now hear what Tristran would do!   **22c**
    Tristran went off; he had made his restitution.
He left the road, taking a track.   3012
He went by trail and by-way
until he came secretly
to the forester's dwelling.
Straightaway, through the entry,   3016
Orri put him into the fine cellar.
He supplied him with whatever he needed.
(Orri was extraordinarily generous;
He would catch boars and sows in snares   3020
and, in his hedges, great stags and does,
deer and roe-deer. He was not stingy with them;
he would give much to his helpers.)
Now Tristran was staying there,   3024
unobserved, underground.
Through Perinis, the noble young man,
Tristran learned news of his beloved.
Hear about the three (may God curse them!)   3028
because of whom Tristran had gone off.
(The king was much maltreated by them.)

Not a full month had passed
before King Marc went hunting   3032
and the traitors with him.
Now listen to what they did that day!
On a heath, to one side,
the villeins had burned out a clearing.   3036
The king halted in the burned area,
hearing the cries of his good dogs.
There the three barons came,
and addressed him.   3040
"King, now attend to our words!
If the queen has been wanton –
she has never formally denied it –
this is said to your shame.   3044
And the barons of your land   **22d**
have many a time entreated you concerning this
because they want her to deny formally
that Tristran ever had her love.   3048
She must clear herself if people are lying about it.
And so have her put to the test,
and straightaway require this of her,
privately, when you retire.   3052
If she does not want to make a formal denial,
let her leave your realm."
   The king, listening, turned red.
"By God! Cornish lords, for a long time   3056
you have not left off laying traps for her.
Here I hear her accused of something
that might well be left alone.
Say if you are aiming   3060
at the queen's going [back] to Ireland.
Each of you, what do you ask of her?
Did not Tristran offer to defend her?
You never dared take up arms in the case.   3064
Because of you he is out of the country.
Now you have quite surprised me.
I have banished him; am I now to banish my wife?
May he have a hundred curses right in the jaw,   3068
the one who asked me to part with him!
By Saint Stephen the Martyr,

you push me too far; it distresses me.
What wonder that a person should grow angry about it!   3072
If he did wrong, he is suffering for it.
You have no care for my well-being;
I can no longer have peace with you.
By Saint Trechmor of Carhaix,   3076
I shall make you a wager:
you will not see Tuesday go by –
today is Monday – before you see him."
The king so frightened them   **23a**   3080
that there was nothing to do but flee.
King Marc said: "May God destroy you,
you who thus go seeking my shame!
You will surely have no profit from it.   3084
I shall summon the baron
whom you put to flight."
Seeing the king displeased,
on the heath, upon a hillock,   3088
all three of them dismounted,
leaving the angry king in the field.
They said among themselves: "What can we do?
King Marc is in a vile mood.   3092
He will may indeed send for his nephew;
not faith nor vow will hold …
If he returns here, it is all over with us.
Neither in forest nor on road   3096
will he find one of us three
without drawing fresh blood from his body.
Let us tell the king: now he will have peace,
we shall never speak to him about this [again]."   3100
    The king remained in the middle of the clearing.
There they came; he promptly rebuffed them,
no longer caring for their speech.
He swore by the faith he held from God,   3104
softly, between his teeth,
that this parley was undertaken to their cost.
If he had reinforcements with him
all three of them, he said, would there be taken prisoner.   3108
"Sire," they said, "hear us.
You are displeased and angry

because we speak of your honour.
By rights one ought to counsel   3112
one's lord; [but] you are ungrateful to us.
Cursed be whatever he has beneath his belt,   **23b**
the one who hates you! That man will depart,
he will be resentful towards you at his peril.   3116
But we, who are your liege-men,
we were giving you loyal counsel.
Since you do not believe us, do as you like;
you will hear us keep very quiet about it.   3120
Put aside this displeasure with us!"
The king listened, saying not a word.
   He had his elbow propped on his saddle-bow
and did not turn towards them in the slightest.   3124
"Lords, it is a very short while ago
that you heard the defence
my nephew made in regard to my wife.
You did not choose to take up a shield.   3128
Go seeking [combat] on foot;
henceforth I bar you from the tournament.
Now leave my whole land!
By Saint Andrew, whom people go seeking   3132
beyond the sea, as far as Scotland,
you have put into my heart a wound
that will not pass away for a year.
Because of you I have banished Tristran."   3136
Before him came the felons,
Godoïne, Ganelon,
and Denoalen, who was very evil.
All three addressed the king   3140
but could not come to terms with him.
Without further stay the king departed.
The others separated from him with ill-will.
They had strong castles, well enclosed by palisades, 3144
seated on rocks and high hills;
they would cause trouble for their lord
if the matter was not amended.
The king lost no time;   **23c**   3148
he did not await dog or huntsman.
At Tintagel he dismounted

in front of his keep; in he went.
No one knew [of his return] or followed him.   3152
He entered the chambers, sword girded.
Iseut rose to greet him,
came towards him, took his sword,
then sat down at his feet.   3156
He took her hand and raised her.
The queen made a reverence to him;
then looked up at him, at his face,
and saw it very cruel and fierce.   3160
She perceived that he was angry,
[and] had come unescorted.
"Alas!" she said [to herself], "my friend
is discovered, my lord has taken him!"   3164
(Softly she said it, between her teeth.)
Her blood was not so slow
that it did not rise to her face.
Her heart turned cold in her chest;   3168
she fainted, her complexion was ashen,
she fell backwards in front of the king,
who raised her in his arms,
kissed her, and embraced her;   3172
he thought that illness had struck her.
When she had recovered from her faint
[he said]: "My dear love, what is the matter?"
"Fear, Sire." "Fear not!"   3176
When she heard him soothing her,
her colour returned and she was sure
that the king was now appeased.
She addressed him affectionately: 3180
"Sire, I see by the colour of your face
that your huntsmen have distressed you.
You must not distress yourself because of the chase."   **23d**
The king heard her, laughed, embraced her,   3184
and said: "Beloved,
    I have three felons who for a long time now
have hated my well-being.
But if I do not yet disown them   3188
[and] drive them out of my land,
they no longer need fear my enmity.

They have always deceived me greatly
and I have given in to them too much.   3192
Changing my mind is not in question henceforth.
Through their speech, through their lies,
I have driven my nephew from me.
I no longer care to deal with them …   3196
He will soon return,
will avenge me on the three felons;
by him they will yet be hanged."
The queen heard this;   3200
she would have spoken aloud, but did not dare.
She was prudent, and so controlled herself,
saying inwardly: "God has done something wonderful
when my lord has become angry   3204
with those through whom an accusation was raised.
I pray God that they may be shamed."
(She said this to herself, so that no one heard it.)
The fair Iseut, who knew how to speak,   3208
said quite innocently to the king:
"Sire, what evil have they said of me?
Everyone can say what he thinks.
Except for you, I have no defender;   3212
this is why they go seeking my harm.
From God, the Spiritual Father,
may they have an evil curse!
They have made me tremble so many times!"   3216
   "Lady," said the king, "now hear me.
Out of ill-will   24a
three of my most valued barons have departed."
"Sire, why? For what reasons?"   3220
"They are accusing you." "Sire, why?"
"I shall tell you," said the king.
"You have not made a formal denial concerning Tristran."
"If I do so?" "And they have told me …   3224
that they have told me." "I am ready for it."
"When will you do it? This very day?"
"You set a short term." "It is long enough."
"Sire, for the sake of God and His names,   3228
   hear me and counsel me.
What can this be? How amazing

that they do not leave me in peace for an hour!
So help me God,   3232
I shall never make them a formal denial
except one that I shall devise.
If I made them an oath,
Sire, in your court, in the sight of your people,   3236
within three days they would tell me
that they would like to have another denial.
King, in this country I have no relative
who, because of my distress,   3240
might make war or rebellion.
But this would suit me very well
(I no longer care about their chatter):
if they want to have my oath,   3244
or if they want a trial by ordeal,
they will not indeed demand a procedure so harsh –
let them set the day! – that I shall not undergo it.
On the day set I shall have, on the spot,   3248
King Arthur and his household.
If I am vindicated before him,
[and] if afterwards anyone wanted to slander me,
those others would make formal denial for me,   3252
those who will have witnessed my defence,   **24b**
against Cornishman or Saxon.
For this reason it suits me well that they should be there
and see my defence with their own eyes.   3256
If Arthur the king is present,
Gawain his nephew, the most courteous,
Girflet and Kay the seneschal –
the king has a hundred such vassals   3260
who will not lie about it for anything they might hear –
they would engage in combat because of slander.
King, this is why it is well
that the defence of my right be made before them.   3264
The Cornish are tale-bearers,
treacherous in many acts.
Set a day, and give them to know
that you want them all   3268
to be at the White Heath, both poor and rich.
Declare clearly that from any who are not there

you will take away their inheritance.
Thus you will be quit of them.   3272
As for myself, I am quite sure
that as soon as King Arthur sees
my messenger, he will come.
I have long known his character."   3276
The king answered: "You have spoken well."
Thereupon the day set was announced
throughout the country: a fortnight hence.
The king made it known to the three natives   3280
who had left the court with ill-will.
They were very glad of it, however it might turn out.
    Now throughout the country all knew
the day fixed for the assembly,   3284
that King Arthur would be there,
and that most of the knights
of his household would come with him.
Iseut wasted no time at all;   **24c**   3288
By Perinis she sent word to Tristran
of all the pain and distress
that she had had, for him, that year.
Might she now reap the reward!   3292
He could, if he would, set her at peace.
"Tell him that he well knows the marsh
at the head of the plank bridge, at the Mal Pas;
there I once soiled my clothes a little.   3296
On the mound, at the head of the plank bridge,
a little on this side of the White Heath,
there let him be, dressed in leper's clothing.
Let him carry with him a hard-wood goblet;   3300
with a leather bottle underneath it,
attached by a knotted thong.
In the other hand let him hold a crutch.
And let him study how to act such a part: 3304
on the appointed day he will be seated on the mound
(his face must be covered with sores);
let him hold up the goblet in front of his forehead;
of those who pass by   3308
let him humbly ask for alms.
They will give him gold and silver.

(He is to keep the money for me until I see him
alone, in a private room.)"   3312
Perinis said: "Lady, in faith,
thus I shall indeed tell him the secret plan."
Perinis left the queen.
Through a thicket he entered the wood   3316
and went through it quite alone.
At dusk he came to the hiding place
where Tristran was, in the fine cellar.
They had got up from eating.   3320
Tristran was glad of his coming;
he well knew that the noble youth
had brought him news of his beloved.
The two held each other by the hand   **24d**   3324
and mounted to a high seat.
Perinis told him
the queen's entire message.
Tristran bent a little towards the ground   3328
and swore by whatever he could think of:
they had plotted this to their own harm; they could not fail
to lose their heads for it
and hang on the gallows, on the cross-pieces.   3332
"Tell the queen, word for word:
I shall go [there] on the day set, let her have no fear.
May she be happy, healthy, and cheerful!
I shall never again have a bath in warm water   3336
until with my sword I have taken revenge
on those who have caused her distress.
They are treacherous, evil men, shown to be so.
Tell her: may she have well devised everything   3340
to save herself from the oath.
I shall see her very soon.
Go, and tell her that she is not to be dismayed,
nor to fear that I shall not go to the judgment,   3344
disguised as a beggar.
King Arthur will indeed see me
sitting at the head [of the plank bridge], at the Mal Pas,
but he will not recognize me.   3348
I shall have his alms, if I can get them out of him.
You can repeat to the queen

what I told you in the stone cellar,
which she made so beautiful.   3352
Take to her from me more greetings
than haws are thick on the hawthorn-tree."
"I shall tell her indeed," said Perinis.
Then he went out by the stairs.   3356
"I am going to King Arthur, fair lord.
I must speak this message to him:
that he is to come to hear the oath,
and with him a hundred knights,   **25a**   3360
who afterwards would vouch for her
if the wicked men should at all grind their teeth
at the lady concerning [her] loyalty.
Is that not well?" "Now go with God!"   3364
He climbed all the steps one by one,
mounted his hunter and went off.
He would have no peace with his spur
until he came to Caerleon.   3368
(He took great pains to serve;
he should be all the better rewarded.)
He kept inquiring about the king
until he was told news reliable and welcome: 3372
that the king was at Snowdon.
Off along the road that leads there
went the squire of Iseut the Fair.
He asked a shepherd playing his reed-pipes,   3376
"Where is the king?"
"Sir," said he, "he sits on the dais.
You will indeed see the Round Table,
which turns like the celestial sphere.   3380
His household sits around it."
Perinis said: "We'll go there, then."
The squire got down at the mounting-block
and immediately went inside.   3384
Within were many counts' sons
and sons of rich sub-vassals,
who were all serving to win arms.
One of them departed, as if fleeing away;   3388
he came to the king, who addressed him:
"Come, what brings you here?" "I bring news:

there outside has come a rider;
he is seeking you urgently."   3392
In came Perinis;
he was watched by many a baron.
He came before the king on the dais,   **25b**
where all of the nobles were seated.   3396
The squire spoke with assurance:
"God save," he said, "King Arthur,
him and all his company,
in the name of the fair Iseut, his friend!"   3400
    The king rose from the tables.
"And may God the Spiritual," he said,
"save and guard her, and you, my friend!
God!" said the king, "I have looked for so long   3404
to have a single message from her!
Young man, in the sight of these barons of mine,
I grant her whatever you request.
You will be made knight, and two others as well,   3408
because of the message of the fairest woman
there is, from here to Tudela."
"Sire," he said, "I thank you!
Hear why I have come;   3412
and let these barons listen attentively
and my lord Gawain in particular.
    The queen has been reconciled
with her lord; this is no secret.   3416
Sire, where they were reconciled
all the barons of the realm were present.
Tristran offered to clear himself
and to defend the queen,   3420
as to her fidelity, before the king.
Yet not one of that body of liege-men
was willing to take up arms.
Sire, now they give King Marc to understand   3424
that he is to hear a defence from her!
There is no nobleman, Frenchman or Saxon,
of her lineage at the king's court.
(I have heard tell that he swims easily,   3428
the man whose chin is supported.)
King, if I am lying about this,   **25c**

take me for a tale-bearer.
The king does not have a firm disposition;   3432
he is now here, now there.
Queen Iseut answered thus:
that she would, before you, justify herself.
At the Perilous Ford –   3436
she asks and entreats
as your dear friend,
that you be there on the day set.
Have there a hundred of your friends,   3440
your household, bound by feudal ties.
She knows your court [to be] so honourable
that if she is cleared before you
(and God guard her, lest it fall out badly!),   3444
afterwards you will be her sureties;
you will in no way fail in this.
The date is set a week from now."
They wept big tears at this;   3448
there was not a single one there who, out of pity,
did not have his face wetted from his eyes.
"God!" said everyone, "what do they ask of her?
The king is doing what they require: 3452
Tristran is leaving the country.
May he never see Holy Paradise,
anyone who, if the king wishes it, will not go there
and who through right will not help her!"   3456
At this Gawain rose to his feet;
he spoke, saying like a courtly man:
"Uncle, if I have your permission,
the trial that has been arranged   3460
will turn out badly for the three felons.
The worst is Ganelon.
I know him well, as he does me.
I thrust him once into a mire   3464
during a vigorous large-scale joust.   **25d**
If I hold him again, by Saint Richier,
Tristran will not need to come there.
If I could get my hands on him   3468
I should cause him much grief
and hang him on a high hill."

Girflet rose after Gawain
and they came forward hand in hand.   3472
"King, they have greatly hated the queen,
Denoalen and Godoïne
and Ganelon, for a very long time.
May God not keep me in my right mind,   3476
if I have an encounter with Godoïne,
[and] if with my great ash lance
I do not pierce his coat of mail,
may I never embrace secretly   3480
a fair lady behind the bed-curtains!"
Perinis, hearing him, bowed his head to him.
Evains, son of Urien, said:
"I know Denoalen well.   3484
He thinks of nothing but accusing people;
he well knows how to befuddle the king.
This much I shall say to him (let him believe it!):
if I encounter him on my path,   3488
as I already did, once before,
may neither law nor faith keep me,
if he cannot defend himself against me,
from hanging him with my two hands!   3492
One must indeed punish a felon.
The king's tale-bearers are playing with him."
    Perinis said to King Arthur:
"Sire, I am sure of this much: 3496
that the felons will get it in the neck,
those who have looked for a quarrel with the queen.
Never was a man threatened at your court,
a man from any distant realm,   **26a**   3500
but you have well dealt with the matter.
In the end they were sorry,
all those who had deserved it."
The king was glad; he flushed a little.   3504
"Sir squire, go and eat.
These men will give thought to avenging her."
The king had great joy in his heart;
he spoke (meaning Perinis to hear him):   3508
"Noble and honoured household,
see to it that, for the meeting day,

your horses all be well fed,
your shields freshly painted, your clothing rich.   3512
We shall joust before the fair one
about whom you all have heard the news.
Little can he love his sweetheart,
the man who will hesitate to bear arms."   3516
    The king had summoned them all.
They hated the day set, because it was so far off;
if they had their wish, it would be tomorrow.
Hear about the nobleman of good birth!   3520
Perinis asked leave [to depart].
The king mounted Passelande,
for he wished to escort the young man.
They went conversing along the way.   3524
All their words were of the fair one
who would cause lances to splinter.
Before the conversation ended,
the king offered to Perinis   3528
the equipment with which to be a knight,
but Perinis did not wish to accept it yet.
The king had escorted him for a while
for the sake of the noble beauty with the blond hair,   3532
in whom there was no ill-will whatsoever;
they spoke about her much as they went along.
The squire had a rich escort   **26b**
of the knights and of the noble king.   3536
It was with much regret that they separated.
The king addressed him: "Good friend,
go off, do not delay.
Greet your lady for me,   3540
on behalf of her own loyal servant,
who is coming to her to make peace.
I shall do every wish of hers.
I shall not be late, for this reason: 3544
she was able, once, to arrive well ahead of me.
Let her recall the throwing of the lance
that was struck into the post;
she will well know where that was.   3548
I pray you to tell her about it in this way."
"King, so I shall do, I promise you."

Thereupon he spurred his hunter;
as for the king, he turned back.   3552
Perinis went on, having delivered
his message, he who had taken such pains
for the queen's service.
He went along as rapidly as he could;   3556
never stopping for a single day
until he came to the place from which he had set out.
He related his expedition
to the lady, who was very glad   3560
on account of [both] King Arthur and Tristran.
That night they were at Lidan.
    That was the tenth night after the new moon.
What should I say? The day set was approaching,   3564
that of the queen's self-exculpation.
Tristran, her lover, was not idle.
He had dressed in an assortment of clothing:
he was in woollen clothes, without a shirt;   3568
his outer garments were of ugly, coarse material
and his boots were patched.   26c
He had had a wide cloak made,
of coarse material, all smoke-blackened.   3572
He had disguised himself very well;
he resembled a leper more than anything else,
and yet he also had his sword
tightly girded about his waist.   3576
Tristran went off; he emerged from the lodging
secretly, with Governal,
who instructed him and told him:
"Lord Tristran, do not be foolish.   3580
Take note of the queen,
for she will give you a hint and a sign."
"Companion," he said, "so I shall do, indeed.
Take care that you do as I wish.   3584
I greatly fear being recognized.
Take my shield and my lance
and bring them to me, and my horse
accoutred, companion Governal.   3588
If I have need, be
at the crossing-place, ready, hidden;

you well know the good crossing,
you have long been familiar with it.   3592
The horse is white as flour;
cover him well all over
so that he may not be recognized
or noticed by anyone.   3596
Arthur will be there with his people
and King Marc likewise.
Those knights from foreign parts
will joust to gain fame;   3600
and for the love of Iseut my beloved
I shall briefly try a venture.
On the lance let there be the pennant,   **26d**
the gift of the fair one.   3604
Companion, go now; I strongly urge
that you do [all] this most carefully."
He picked up his goblet and his crutch.
Having taken leave of him and received it,   3608
Governal came to his lodging,
Did nothing but take his equipment,
then quickly set out on the way.
He did not wish to be seen by anyone.   3612
He travelled until he concealed himself
near Tristran, who was at the Mal Pas.
On a mound, at the edge of the marsh,
Tristran sat down without more ado.   3616
In front of him he planted his crutch;
it was attached to a thong
by which he had hung it from his neck.
Around him were the soft, marshy places.   3620
He drew himself well up onto the mound.
He did not resemble a crippled man,
for he was large and well-fleshed;
he was not a dwarf, a cripple, or a hunchback.   3624
He heard the throng; there he sat down.
He had well covered his face with sores.
When someone passed before him
he would say, moaning: "Woe is me!   3628
I never thought to be a beggar
or serve in this calling for a single day.

But now there is nothing else I can do."
Tristran made them dip into their purses;   3632
he managed to make everyone give him something.
He received [the alms] without making any comment.
(A man who has been a beggar for seven years
is not so skilful at extracting money from people.)   3636
Even the errand-runners
and the least among the serving-boys,
who went eating along the way –
Tristran, keeping his head bowed,   **27a**   3640
asked their alms for God's sake.
One would give him something, another would strike him.
The low-born boys, devoid of faith,
called him beggar, good-for-nothing.   3644
Tristran listened, spoke no word [in retaliation],
saying only that for God's sake he forgave them.
The "crows," who were full of rage,
plagued him; yet he was prudent.   3648
They called him vagabond and good-for-nothing.
He helped them along with his crutch,
making more than fourteen of them bleed
so much that they could not stanch it.   3652
The well-bred young men of good family
gave him farthings or silver half-pennies;
which he accepted;
He told them that he would drink to them all.   3656
He had so great a burning in his body,
he could scarcely get rid of it.
All those who heard him speak so
took to weeping out of pity.   3660
Not in the slightest did they suspect,
they who saw him, that he was not a leper.
[Before him] passed serving-men and squires
hastening to unburden themselves [of their loads]   3664
and to set up the tents for their lords,
pavilions of many colours.
(There was no rich man there who did not have his tent.)
At full speed, by road and path,   3668
the knights came after them.
There was a very great crowd in that marsh;

they sank in (the mud was soft).
The horses went in up to their flanks;   3672
many a one fell in, even if others dragged themselves out.
Tristran laughed at this; he was not at all dismayed.
Mischievously, he said to them all: 27b
"Hold your reins by the knots   3676
and strike well with the spur;
for God's sake, spur on,
for there is no mud up ahead."
When they thought to try (the footing) beyond,   3680
the marshy ground sank beneath their [horses'] feet.
Everyone who entered was muddied;
the man who had no boots felt the lack of them.
The "leper" drew out his hand;   3684
when he saw one of them wallowing in the mire,
then he would rattle away vigorously.
When he saw him deepest in the mud
the "leper" would say: "Think of me!   3688
May God bring you out of the Mal Pas!
Help [me] to get some new clothes!"
With his bottle he struck the goblet.
(He was begging of them in an odd place,   3692
but he did it in sport,
so that when he saw his beloved pass by,
Iseut with the blond hair,
she might have joy at it in her heart.)   3696
There was a great uproar in this Mal Pas.
Those who crossed it soiled their clothes;
from far away one could hear the cries
of those getting soiled by the bog.   3700
No one crossing it was safe.
At that point, here was King Arthur.
He came to watch the crossing,
many of his barons with him.   3704
They feared that the marsh might sink [beneath them].
All the men of the Round Table
had come to the Mal Pas
with fresh shields and well-fed horses,   3708
identified by their coats of arms.
They were all in armour, hand and foot.   27c

Many a silken banner was raised there.
They went jousting before the ford.   3712
Tristran well recognized King
Arthur, and called him over:
"Lord Arthur, King, I am sick,
sore-covered, leprous, infirm, and feeble.   3716
My father is poor, never had land.
I have come here to seek alms.
I have heard much good spoken of you;
you should not refuse me.   3720
You are dressed in fine grey cloth –
from Regensburg, I think.
Under the linen from Rheims
your flesh is white and smooth.   3724
I see your legs covered
with fine silken cloth and green mesh,
and gaiters of fine, dyed woollen cloth.
King Arthur, see how I scratch myself!   3728
I am very cold, whoever may be warm.
For God's sake give me those gaiters!"
The noble king felt pity for him;
two young men removed his gaiters.   3732
The "sick man" took them,
put them on quickly,
and sat down again on the mound.
The "leper" spared none of those   3736
who passed before him;
he got from them fine clothes in plenty
as well as King Arthur's gaiters.
Tristran sat down above the marsh.   3740
When he had installed himself there,
King Marc, proud and powerful,
came riding hard towards the bog.
Tristran undertook to see   3744
whether he could get anything out of him.   **27d**
He sounded his rattle loudly;
with his hoarse voice he cried out with effort,
making his breath whistle through his nose: 3748
"For God's sake, King Marc, a little something!"
[Marc] pulled off his fur-trimmed hood, and said: "Here,

brother, put this on your head!
Many a time the weather has been hard on you."   3752
"Sire," he says, "I thank you!
Now you have protected me from the cold."
He put the hood under his cloak,
folding and hiding it as well as he could.   3756
"Where are you from, leper?" said the king.
"From Caerleon, the son of a Welshman."
"How many years have you been away from society?"
"Sire, it has been three years, truly.   3760
While I was in good health
I had a very courtly sweetheart.
Because of her I have these large sores.
These smoothly planed clappers,   3764
it is she who makes me sound them night and day
and with the noise deafen
all those of whom I ask something of theirs
for the love of God the Creator."   3768
The king said to him: "Do not conceal
how your sweetheart gave it to you."
"Lord King, her husband was a leper.
I took my pleasure with her;   3772
through our congress this illness seized me.
But there was never a woman more beautiful, save one."
"Who is she?" "The fair Iseut;
she dresses as [the other one] used to do."   3776
Hearing this, the king parted from him laughing.
From the other side, King Arthur,
who had been jousting, came up.
He was as happy as he could be.   **28a**   3780
Arthur inquired about the queen.
"She is coming," said Marc, "through the woods,
Lord King; she comes with Andret;
he has undertaken to escort her."   3784
One of them said to another: "I do not know
how she may get out of this Mal Pas.
Now let us stay here and watch closely."
The three felons (may an evil fire burn them!)   3788
came to the ford and asked
of the leper where they had crossed,

the ones who got least muddy.
Tristran raised his crutch   3792
and pointed out a big quagmire to them.
"Do you see the peat-bog beyond that mire?
There is the true landmark;
I have seen many people cross there."   3796
The felons entered the mud
where the "leper" directed them.
They found mud in great plenty,
up to the sides of their saddles.   3800
All three fell in together.
The "leper" was above on the mound
and called to them: "Spur hard
if you are muddied by such a bog!   3804
Come, lords! By the holy Apostle,
give me something of yours, each of you!"
The horses sank into the mire;
those men began to be dismayed   3808
because they found neither bank nor bottom.
Those who were jousting on the high ground
came running swiftly.
Hear about the "leper," how he lied!   3812
"Lords," he said to those [three] barons,
"hold on well to your saddle-bows!
A curse on this marsh that is so soft!   28b
Take off those cloaks from your necks   3816
and swim through the mire!
I am telling you what I very well know:
I have seen people cross here today."
You should have seen the goblet being struck!   3820
When the "leper" shook the goblet,
he struck the bottle with the thong,
and with the other hand he rattled away.
Thereupon the fair Iseut arrived.   3824
She saw her enemies in the mire,
her lover sitting on the mound.
At this she was most joyful; she laughed and was gay.
She dismounted on the bank.   3828
On the other side were the kings
and the barons they had with them,

who were watching those in the mire
turn now on their sides, now on their bellies.   3832
And the "leper" urged them on:
"Lords, the queen has come
to make her defence.
Go to hear this trial."   3836
There were few there who were not glad at this.
Hear about the "leper," the deformed man!
He addressed Denoalen:
"Put your hand on my stick;   3840
pull hard with both fists!"
[The other man] immediately reached for it.
The "leper," on purpose, let go of the stick;
[the other man] fell back, and submerged entirely;   3844
nothing was seen of him but his hair sticking up.
And when he was dragged out of the mire,
the "leper" said: "I could do no more;
I have numb joints and nerves,   3848
hands benumbed with some affliction,
feet swollen from gout.   **28c**
The sickness has diminished my strength;
my arms are shrivelled like tree-bark."   3852
   Dinas was positioned near the queen;
he grasped the situation, winked at her.
He well knew that it was Tristran under the cloak;
he saw the three felons in the trap.   3856
For him this was good; it pleased him much
that they were in an ugly situation.
With great difficulty and with pain
the accusers emerged   3860
from the mire; certainly
they would never again be clean without a bath.
In the sight of the crowd they undressed,
left their clothes and put on others.   3864
But now hear about the noble Dinas,
who was on the other side of the Pas!
He addressed the queen:
"Lady, he said, "that rich cloak   3868
will be quite ruined.
This marsh is full of slime.

I am sorry, it grieves me much
if a jot of it should cling to your clothes."   3872
Iseut laughed, undaunted;
she winked at him and then stared.
He knew the queen's thought.
A bit lower down, near a thorn-bush,   3876
he turned towards a ford, he and Andret,
where they crossed fairly clean.
On the near side was Iseut, alone.
In front of the ford the crowd   3880
of the kings and their barons was great.
Hear how clever Iseut was!
She well knew that they were watching her,
those who were positioned beyond the Mal Pas   3884
She came up to the palfrey,   **28d**
took the straps of the saddle-cloth,
knotted them over the saddle-bows.
No squire or serving-man   3888
would have raised them better because of the mire
or arranged them better.
She, fair Iseut, pushed the reins under the saddle,
removed the breast-strap,   3892
removed the bit from the palfrey.
She held up her dress with one hand,
held the riding-crop with the other.
She came to the ford with the palfrey.   3896
She struck it with the crop,
and it crossed over beyond the marsh.
    The queen had the full attention
of those who were on the other side.   3900
The renowned kings were amazed at [her actions],
as were all the others who were watching.
The queen had silken clothes;
they had been brought from Baghdad   3904
and were lined with white ermine.
Mantle, tunic – it all dragged on the ground.
Her hair, on her shoulders,
was bound with linen bands over pure gold.   3908
On her head she had a golden circlet
which went all the way round;

her complexion [was] rosy, fresh, and fair.
Thus she made for the wooden walkway.   3912
"I want to have to do with you."
"Noble queen of high birth,
I shall go to you without refusal
but I don't know what you have in mind."   3916
"I do not wish to muddy my clothes;
you will be a donkey to carry me
very carefully across [by] the walkway."
"No!" he said, "noble Queen,   29a   3920
ask no such service of me.
I am a leper, full of sores, deformed."
"Quick," said she, "position yourself a little!
Do you think that your sickness will infect me?   3924
Have no fear, it will not."
"Ah, God!" he said, "what will come of this?
I do not at all mind talking to her."
[He approached], leaning heavily on his crutch.   3928
"Well! Sick man, you are very large!
Turn your face that way and your back this way;
I shall mount like a boy."
And then the "leper" smiled at that;   3932
he turned his back, and she mounted.
They were all watching, kings and counts.
He held her thighs over his crutch,
raised one foot and limped with the other,   3936
often seemed about to fall;
he made a great show of suffering.
The fair Iseut rode,
one leg on each side.   3940
One person said to the other: "Now look
. . . . .
see the queen bestride
a sick man whom she causes to limp!   3944
He is nearly falling from the walkway,
holding his crutch under her hip.
Let us go to meet that leper
at the edge of this marsh!"   3948
The young squires ran there
. . . . .

King Arthur moved in that direction,
and the others all in order.   3952
The "leper" had his face lowered;
he came to [solid] ground on the other side.
Iseut let herself slip down;
The "leper" prepared to go back.   3956
At the point of leaving, in exchange, he asked of her,   **29b**
the fair Iseut, some food for that night.
Arthur said: "He has well earned it.
Ah! Queen, give it to him!"   3960
The fair Iseut said to the king:
"By that faith that I owe you,
he is a strong rascal, he has plenty;
he will not eat today what he [already] has.   3964
Under his cloak I felt his belt.
King, his scrip does not grow smaller:
half-loaves and whole ones
and pieces and quarter-loaves –   3968
I felt them well through the bag.
He has food, and he is well clothed.
For your gaiters, if he wants to sell them,
he can get five sterling *sous*.   3972
And with my husband's hood
let him buy sheep and be a shepherd,
or [buy] a donkey that can cross the marsh.
He is a good-for-nothing, that I know.   3976
Today he has obtained good pickings,
has found people to his measure.
From me he will not take away anything worth
a single farthing or a penny."   3980
The two kings were greatly amused by this.
They had her palfrey brought up
and helped her to mount, then they [all] turned away.
Those who had arms then engaged in jousting.   3984
Tristran moved away from the assembly
and came to his companion, who was awaiting him.
He had brought two valuable Castilian horses,
bridled and saddled,   3988
and two lances and two shields
(he had disguised them very well).

What should I tell you about the riders?
Governal had put a white silken scarf   **29c**   3992
over his head;
nothing of it showed except the eye[s].
He turned away rapidly;
he had a very handsome, well-fed horse.   3996
As for Tristran, he had Bel Joëor;
one could find no better.
Its sides and loins, the stirrups and the shield –
all this was covered with a heavy black cloth.   4000
Its face was covered with a black veil;
it had both head and coat covered.
On his lance [Tristran] had placed the pennon
that the fair one had sent him.   4004
Each man bestrode his war horse;
each had his steel sword girded on.
So armed, on their horses,
through a green meadow between two valleys   4008
they burst upon the Blanche Lande.
Gawain, Arthur's nephew, asked
of Girflet: "Do you see two of them,
there, coming at full speed?   4012
I don't recognize them; do you know who they are?"
"I recognize them well," answered Girflet.
"One has a black horse and a black pennon:
that is the Black Knight of the Mountain.   4016
I know the other by the variegated arms,
for in this country there are scarcely any such.
They are enchanted, I have no doubt of that."
These men turned aside from the track,   4020
shields in hand, lances raised,
pennons fixed to the iron tips.
They carried their equipment as well
as if they had been born inside it.   4024
   King Marc and King Arthur spoke
much more of those two
than they did of their [own] two companies   **29d**
that were yonder in the broad plains.   4028
The two [riders] repeatedly appeared in the lists
and were watched by many people.

They spurred together through the outposts
but found no one with whom they might join in combat.   4032
The queen recognized them well;
she was stationed to one side of the lists,
she and Brengain. And Andret came
on his war horse; he bore his arms.   4036
Lance raised, shield gripped,
he attacked Tristran head-on.
He did not at all recognize him,
but Tristran knew him well.   4040
He struck his shield; onto the pathway
he brought him down, arm shattered.
He lay before the queen's feet
on his back, without rising.   4044
Governal saw the forester
coming from the tents, on a war horse –
the one who had tried to deliver Tristran to death
in the forest, where he was sound asleep.   4048
[Governal] headed at great speed
towards the man who would be in deadly peril.
He put the sharp iron into his body;
along with the steel he pushed out the leather [lacing].   4052
That man fell dead so quickly that never did a priest
come in time, nor could one have been there.
Iseut, who was noble and frank,
laughed at this softly, beneath her wimple.   4056
Girflet, Cinglor, Evains,
Tolas, Coris, and Gawain
saw their companions disgraced.
"Lords," said Gawain, "what shall we do?   4060
There lies the forester, open-mouthed.
Be sure that those two are enchanted.   **30a**
We do not recognize them in the slightest.
Now they hold us to be fools.   4064
Let's spur towards them, let's go capture them!"
"He who can deliver them to us," said the king,
"will have served us very much to our satisfaction."
Tristran drew away down towards the ford,   4068
Governal also; they passed over.
The others dared not follow them;

they stayed still, gripped by fear,
thinking indeed that it was an enchantment.   4072
They wished to return to their lodgings,
for they had left off jousting.
   Arthur led off the queen, on his right.
The way seemed very short to him   4076
. . . . .
which would depart from the way, to the right.
They dismounted at their lodgings.
There were many of these on the heath;   4080
the tent-ropes cost a great deal.
In place of reeds and rushes
they had all strewn their tents with flowers.
They came by roads and by paths.   4084
The Blanche Lande was crowded;
many a knight had his beloved there.
Anyone who was there in the meadow
heard horns sounding the pursuit of many great stags.   4088
That night they stayed on the heath.
Each king held a session to hear pleas.
Whoever had means was not slow:
one person made presents to another.   4092
After eating, King Arthur
went to King Marc's tent to pay a visit,
taking along his immediate household.
There were few woollen garments there;   4096
most of them were of silk.
What should I say about the clothes?   **30b**
What wool there was, was dyed;
that woollen cloth [was] richly coloured.   4100
There were many people finely dressed;
no one [ever] saw two richer courts;
nothing needful was lacking.
In the pavilions they made merry.   4104
That night they discussed their business:
how the noble, well-born lady
was to defend herself against the accusation
in the sight of the kings and their barons.   4108
King Arthur went off to bed
with his barons and his close friends.

Many a reed-pipe, many a trumpet –
anyone who was in the woods that night   4112
would have heard them sounding in the pavilions.
Before daybreak it began to thunder:
it was a sure sign of heat to come.
The watchmen sounded the [new] day;   4116
everywhere people began to get up,
they all arose without delay.
   The sun was warm by Prime;
both mist and dew had disappeared.   4120
Before the tents of the two kings
the Cornish people assembled.
There was no knight in all the kingdom
who did not have his wife at court with him.   4124
A silken cloth with a dark brocade
was placed before the king's tent.
It was spread out on the green grass,
finely worked with [figures of] animals.   4128
(The cloth was bought in Nicaea).
In Cornwall there were no relics
in treasury or phylacteries,
in chests or other containers,   4132
in reliquaries, jewel-boxes, or shrines,   **30c**
in crosses of gold or silver, or in maces,
that had not been placed on the brocade,
arranged and set in order.   4136
The kings drew to one side;
there they wished to make a fair judgment.
The first to speak was King Arthur,
who was a ready speaker.   4140
"King Marc," he says, "whoever urges you
to such an outrageous act, such an amazing thing –
surely that man acts disloyally.
You are easy to persuade;   4144
you ought not to believe false words.
He was making you a very bitter sauce,
the one who caused you to call this assembly.
He ought to pay very dearly   4148
and suffer for it, the one who wanted to do this.
The noble Iseut, the well-born lady,

wants no respite or [other] day set.
They may know, of a surety, 4152
those who will come to hear her defence,
that I shall yet have them hanged,
those who will accuse her of infidelity
after her defence, out of spite. 4156
They would be deserving of death.
Now you will hear, King, who is in the wrong.
The queen will come forward
so that great and humble will see her, 4160
and she will swear, with her right hand
upon the relics, to the Heavenly King
that never did she have a shared love
with your nephew, in any degree whatsoever, 4164
which anyone might think shameful,
nor did she engage in lustful love.
Lord Marc, this has gone on too long.
When she has sworn thus, **30d** 4168
tell your barons to hold their peace."
"Ah! Lord Arthur, what more can I do?
You blame me, and you are right,
for a man who believes envious people is a fool. 4172
I have believed them beyond my inclination.
If the defence is in this meadow,
there will never be a man so bold,
if after the denials 4176
he said anything dishonourable about her,
that he would not receive an ill reward.
Know this, Arthur, noble King
what has been done is against my will. 4180
Now let them take care from this day onwards!"
With that, they ended the consultation.
    They all sat down in rows,
except for the two kings, as was right; 4184
Iseut was between the two of them, her hands in theirs.
Gawain was near the relics.
Arthur's well-esteemed household
was positioned around the brocade. 4188
Arthur took the proceedings in hand,
he who was closer to Iseut,

"Listen to me, fair Iseut;
hear what you are called to affirm: 4192
that Tristran had towards you no love
[marked by] debauchery or infidelity,
nothing but that love that he was duty-bound to have
towards his uncle and his [uncle's] wife."   4196
   "Lords," she said, "thanks be to God!
Here I see holy relics.
Listen now to what I swear here,
by which I affirm to the king here present –   4200
so help me God and Saint Hilaire,
these relics, this reliquary,
and all those [relics] that are not here   **31a**
and all those [reliquaries] throughout the world –   4204
that between my thighs no man has entered
except for the leper for whom I made a heavy load,
who carried me beyond the fords,
and King Marc my spouse.   4208
These two I except from my oath;
I except no one else, of all people.
Concerning two men I cannot exonerate myself:
the leper, and King Marc my lord.   4212
The leper was between my legs
. . . . .
If anyone wants me to do more,
I am quite ready, in this place."   4216
   All those who heard her swear
could endure it no longer.
"God!" said each of them, "so harsh an injustice!
So much has she has done afterwards as justification!   4220
She has put more into it than the felons said
and than they required.
She needs to make no further defence
than you have heard, the great and the humble,   4224
as well as the king and his nephew.
She has sworn and made a vow
that between her thighs no man has entered
save the leper who carried her   4228
yesterday, around Terce, beyond the fords,
and King Marc, her spouse.

A curse on anyone who will ever doubt her on this!"
Arthur's nephew rose to his feet;   4232
he addressed King Marc
so that all the barons heard him:
"King, we have seen the defence
and heard it and listened to it well   4236
Now let the three felons take care,
Denoalen and Ganelon
and the evil Godoïne,   **31b**
never to speak of it, not once.   4240
I should never be in any land
where peace or war might hold me,
as soon as I should hear news
from Queen Iseut the fair,   4244
from spurring to her
to defend her, most rightly."
"Sir," she said, "I thank you!"
The three men were much hated at court.   4248
The courts separated and went off.
The fair Iseut with the blond hair
greatly thanked King Arthur.
"Lady," he said, "I assure you: 4252
you will never again find anyone who might say to you
(as long as I may have health or life)
a single thing not to your honour.
The felons contrived this for their own downfall.   4256
I pray the king your lord,
faithfully and very much out of love,
never again to believe a felon concerning you."
King Marc said: "If I should do so   4260
henceforth, then censure me."
One king separated from the other;
each came away into his own kingdom.
King Arthur went off to Durham;   4264
King Marc remained in Cornwall.
Tristran stayed [where he was], his mind at ease.
    The king held Cornwall in peace;
all feared him, both far and near.   4268
He took Iseut along in his pastimes,
exerting himself to show love to her.

But whoever might be at peace, the three felons
were intent upon treachery.   4272
To them there came a spy
who was seeking to change his [condition in] life.   **31c**
"Lords," said he, "now listen to me!
If I lie to you, then hang me!   4276
The other day the king was displeased with you
and took to hating you
because of his wife's defence.
I allow you to hang me or exile me   4280
if I do not show you, plainly,
Tristran, where he awaits his opportunity
to speak with his dear mistress.
He is in hiding, and I know the place.   4284
(Tristran knows much about Malpertuis.)
When the king goes off to his pastimes,
[Tristran] goes into the chamber – to 'take leave.'
Make ashes of me in a fire,   4288
if you go to the window
of the chamber, in back, to the right,
if you do not see Tristran come,
his sword girded, holding a bow,   4292
two arrows in the other hand.
This night you will see him come, towards dawn."
"How do you know this?" "I have seen him."
"Tristran?" "Indeed, and recognized [him]."   4296
"When was he there?" "I saw him there this morning."
"And who with him?" "That friend of his."
"Friend? And who?" "Lord Governal."
"Where have they put themselves?" "They are at ease   4300
in fine lodgings." "It's at Dinas's home?"
"What do I know?" "They are not there
unbeknownst to him." "That may well be."
"Where shall we see him?" "Through the window   4304
of the chamber; this is quite true.
If I show him to you, I must have a great reward
for it, as much as I expect."
"Name the price." "One silver mark."   4308
"And much more than is promised,   **31d**
so help us Church and Mass!

If you point him out [to us], you cannot fail
of our making you rich."   4312
   "Now listen to me," said the scoundrel.
"There is a small opening
just where the queen's chamber is.
The curtain goes in front of it.   4316
Behind the chamber the stream is wide
and the irises very thick.
Let one of you three go there early.
Through the gap in the new garden   4320
let him go quietly up to the opening.
(making sure to keep to the left).
With a knife, make a long stick,
sharply pointed.   4324
Prick the cloth of the curtain
with the sharp thorn-twig.
Let him carefully push aside the curtain
at the opening [being sure that no one notices],   4328
so that you may see in clearly
when he comes to speak to her.
If you keep watch so, for just three days,
I agree to being burned   4332
if you do not see what I am telling you."
Each of them said: "I promise you
to keep our agreement."
They sent the spy ahead.   4336
   Then they discussed which of the three of them
would go first to see the love-making
that Tristran carried on in the chamber
with her who was his entirely.   4340
They agreed that Godoïne
would go on the first occasion.
They separated, each going his own way;
tomorrow they would know how Tristran behaved.   **32a**   4344
God! The noble woman was not on her guard
against the felons and their intrigue.
By Perinis, a trusted servant,
she had sent word that on the next day   4348
Tristran should come to her early
(the king was to go to Saint Lubin).

Lords, now hear something amazing!
On the next day the night was dusky. 4352
Tristran had set out on the way
through the dense part of a clump of thorn-trees
At the edge of a wood
he looked about, [and] saw Godoïne, 4356
who was coming from his hiding-place.
Tristran made an ambush for him;
concealing himself in the thicket.
"Ah, God!" he said, "look upon me! 4360
May the man who is coming not notice me
until I have him in front of me!"
He awaited him at a distance, holding his sword.
[But] Godoïne took another path. 4364
Tristran remained where he was, highly vexed at this.
He emerged from the thicket and moved in that direction,
but to no avail, for the other man was drawing away,
the one who had set his mind on evil-doing. 4368
Tristran looked into the distance, and saw –
only a short time had elapsed –
Denoalen come ambling along
with two very large greyhounds. 4372
   [Tristran] took his stand against an apple tree.
Denoalen came along the path
on a little black palfrey.
He had sent his dogs to start 4376
a fierce boar in a thicket.
(Before they could flush him out
their master would have got such a blow on the neck   **32b**
as would never be healed by a physician.) 4380
The valiant Tristran was free of his cloak.
Denoalen approached rapidly;
He suspected nothing before Tristran jumped out.
He tried to flee, but failed; 4384
Tristran was too close before him.
He killed him. What else could he do?
[Denoalen] was seeking his death; [Tristran] warded it off,
for he severed the head from the trunk. 4388
[Denoalen] had no time to say: "You are wounding me!"

With his sword [Tristran] cut off his tresses
and stuffed them into his hose.
(When he would show them to Iseut   4392
let her thereby believe that he had killed him!)
Tristran departed from there rapidly.
"Alas!" he said, "what has become
of Godoïne? Where has he gone,   4396
he whom I saw coming so swiftly just now?
Has he passed by? Did he suddenly turn aside?
If he had awaited me, he might have learned
that he would have no better reward   4400
than the one that Denoalen, the felon, carries away,
he to whom I left his lifeless head."
Tristran left the body lying
on the heath, on its back, bleeding.   4404
He wiped his sword and put it back
in its sheath; he took up his cloak
and put the hood over his head.
He dragged a great branch over the body.   4408
He came to his lover's chamber –
But now hear how it befell him!
Godoïne had come running
and had arrived before Tristran.   4412
He had pricked the curtain within [the opening];
he saw the chamber, which was strewn with reeds,   **32c**
saw all that there was in it,
saw no man but Perinis.   4416
He saw Brengain, the young lady, there
where she had combed the hair of fair Iseut.
She still had the comb with her.
The felon who was at the wall   4420
looked, and saw Tristran enter,
holding a bow of solid laburnum wood.
In his hand he held his two arrows,
in the other, two long tresses.   4424
He doffed his cloak; his fine body appeared.
Fair Iseut with the golden hair
rose before him and greeted him.
Through her window she saw the shadow   4428

of the head of Godoïne.
The queen kept her wits about her
([although] her whole body broke into an angry sweat.)
Tristran spoke to Iseut [of what he had brought]:   4432
"So may God keep me," he said, "as His own,
here are the tresses of Denoalen;
I have avenged you on him.
Never[more] will shield or lance   4436
be bought or be utilized by him."
"Sir," she said, "what is that to me?
But I ask you to bend that bow,
and we shall see how it is strung."   4440
Tristran stood still, and took thought.
Listen! He wrestled in his mind;
he took his decision, and bent the bow.
He asked for news of King Marc;   4444
Iseut told him what she knew.

. . . . .

(If [the observer] could escape this alive,
he would, on the matter of King Marc and Iseut his wife,   4448
make deadly war break out anew.
[Tristran], God grant that he win honour!   **32d**
will keep him from escaping.)
Iseut had no interest in chatting.   4452
"Friend, nock an arrow;
take care that the string doesn't tangle.
I see something that troubles me.
Tristran, draw your bow for us."   4456
Tristran stood still, thought briefly;
he well knew that she saw something
that displeased her. He looked up,
was fear-stricken, trembled and started: 4460
against the light, through the curtain,
he saw Godoïne's head.
"Ah! God, true king, so many fine shots
have I made with bow and arrow.   4464
Grant me that this one not miss!
One of the three scoundrels of Cornwall
do I see, up to no good, there outside.
God, who gave Thy most holy body   4468

over to death for humanity,
let me have vengeance for the wrong
these scoundrels direct against me!"
Then he turned towards the wall;   4472
he had his bow drawn, and he shot.
The arrow flew so fast,
nothing could have escaped it.
He made it streak through [Godoïne's] eye,   4476
it pierced his skull and his brain.
Neither hawk nor swallow
flies half so rapidly;
if [the head] had been a rotten apple   4480
the arrow would not have gone through it more swiftly.
The man fell and struck a post,
never moving feet or arms.
He did not even have time to say: 4484
   "I'm wounded! God! Confession …"

Notes

NB. Throughout these notes, unless further expanded upon, "Reid" refers to a note in his *The "Tristran" of Béroul: A Textual Commentary*; "Braet/Raynaud de Lage II" refers to their *Notes et Commentaires*, the second volume of their *Béroul, Tristran et Iseut*; likewise citations from "Ewert," "Gregory," "Jonin," and "Varvaro" designate their respective editions and translations. All of these works are listed in parts 1 and 2 of the Bibliography.

2 This is the beginning of the first preserved folio; it starts in mid-sentence and mid-couplet. The scene brings together the three main characters.

5–28 On the challenges presented by the opening folios, and particularly this one, see the Notes to the Critical Edition.

5f Iseut forestalls Tristran by her first words, "**Sire Tristran**," distant and formal (thus also in 21 and 85, **Sire** alone in 31, 41, 79, 163, but merely **Tristran** in 18, 60, 69, 92, 172, 186, 219). These repetitions in the course of her long speech serve as a warning to him, and establish at the outset the tone of the playlet they are to improvise. (Their understanding is confirmed in 97–100.) See also Ewert's interpretation of the opening episode, II, 69, 75–9.

7 The whole scene is played out at night; the dwarf Frocin soon will learn of Marc's rage against him by looking up at the stars (321–31).

8 Earlier editors have deciphered **fait senblant con s'ele plore** ("she pretends to weep").

17–19 Iseut implies that Tristran has never before been granted a private meeting. Tristran will confirm this, 103–5, mentioning earlier requests.

20–5 This oath, taken before God and two human listeners (who will understand it very differently), anticipates the equally ambiguous defence that Iseut will make later, 4197–4216. Oaths and truth-claims, very frequently with God called to witness them, will form a recurrent motif throughout the poem.

24–5 The first double entendre in the fragment, meant to deceive the listening Marc, who is ignorant of the beginning of Iseut's love affair with his nephew during the voyage from Ireland to Cornwall prior to her marriage. (This episode may of course have been related in the initial, lost portion of Béroul's poem. It is preserved in other twelfth- and thirteenth-century redactions, e.g., that of Gottfried von Strassburg, who has Iseut's maid substituting for her mistress on Marc's wedding night.) What Iseut says here is literally true, and serves as introduction to her modus operandi throughout. There is a similar equivocation at 37–8: **seignor** often means "husband," but also signifies "lord."

26–8 When the Morholt, Iseut's uncle, came demanding a tribute of Cornish children (see 848–57), no Cornish baron but only Tristran (Marc's nephew, and yet a foreigner) dared to challenge him. The episodes preceding Béroul's fragment are found in other sources; see Ewert II, 36–46.

32–4 This statement encapsulates Iseut's chief concern: to avoid public disgrace.

40 Lit.: "from high, so low!" (an allusion to the Wheel of Fortune; see Morawski #764).

50–3 In other accounts (e.g., Eilhart von Oberge's, drawing on a source perhaps also known to Béroul), Tristran, wounded by the Morholt's poisoned spear, eventually drifted in an open boat to Ireland and there was healed by Iseut or her mother. Béroul makes Iseut herself the healer.

58–9 These lines are problematical. Ewert argues persuasively for taking 58 as exclamatory; but see Sandqvist, who tentatively emends it to "S'il veoient Deu …" From Muret onwards, scholars have taken 59 as referring to Jeremiah 18:17: "Dorsum et non faciem ostendam eis in die perditionis eorum" (see M^4 p. 163; in the Douay version, "I will shew them the back and not the face, in the day of their destruction"); but Jeremiah is a rather strained allusion for Iseut to make. It should also be noted (but has not been, heretofore) that Béroul mentions no back. In fact, the theme of seeing God face to face occurs often in the Old Testament, beginning with Genesis 32:30.

103–5 These lines confirm 17–19 and 60–3. (We need not take them as factual.)

104 As a trusted retainer, Tristran not only had entrée into the royal chamber but also slept there (before being expelled from it), in this rather simple court. After Marc's suspicions are allayed, Tristran will take to sleeping there again (569–72).

118–24 The felons' perennial hostility to Tristran is never explained in the fragments of Béroul or Béroul II.

124–5 Tristran is Marc's nephew, a very close relationship in this period. If Marc should die without issue, Tristran could be a claimant to the throne.

135–42 Echoing Iseut's allusion in 26–8, Tristran rehearses for Marc's benefit and at greater length his slaying of the Morholt, thereby reminding Marc of his debt to himself.

161 "Across the sea": there is no indication of which sea, nor of which land he had left. Clearly Tristran is not a native of Cornwall; he twice mentions the possibility of going to **Loinois/Loinoi** (2310, 2868, now usually identified as Lothian in southeastern Scotland) if he should leave Cornwall.

204 Banished from the royal apartment (his former sleeping-place, 104), Tristran has been reduced to taking lodging in the town, has consequently incurred debts, and has left his equipment (except for his indispensable sword) as surety. See note on 3609.

211–15 An obscure passage (and 213 is syntactically imprenetrable, hence my emendation). Ewert translates: "I never had anything belonging to King Mark and even if I did, my uncle would wish before the year is out that he had never harboured such a thought, even at the price of his own weight in gold." See Braet/Raynaud de Lage II. Gregory takes 213–14 as referring to the past.

235–7 The **perron** with definite article is not easy to identify. The word often means "mounting-block," but this hardly belongs in a garden. Perhaps "edge of the fountain" or "stone bench"?

237 tot sol: quite alone. Tristran's soliloquy is in fact directed at the hidden listener.

238 Saint Evrol (ms.: **evtol** or **eutol**): St Ebrulfus of Bayeux, venerated in Normandy.

248 Ms.: **hom nu**. A knight was "naked" without his arms and armour. That he normally carried his sword or had it close by him was taken for granted. Tristran will be seized in his bed and sent swordless (1009) to his execution; Governal's bringing both weapon and body-armour (971–1016), and riding a horse (966, 1245), will make all the difference.

264 (et passim). **Tintaguel/Tintajol**. A residence of King Marc, located on the northwest coast of Cornwall, some thirty miles from the Mal Pas in southwest Cornwall. See Ditmas, "The Invention of Tintagel," 131–6.

265–80 Is this passage to be taken as an interior monologue, or an audible soliloquy?

277–84 A story current in the Middle Ages (see Ewert II). The analogy with Marc's situation is strained: Frocin is in Marc's mind the queen's false accuser, not her lover, and in the anecdote as related here the dwarf Segoçon is castrated, whereas the punishment of the empress is only hinted at (284). Unlike other editors, who put quotation marks after 284, I take 281–4 not as part of Marc's soliloquy but as an authorial sequel to the king's speech. It is most implausible psychologically that Marc, newly convinced of having been induced to believe a lie about his nephew and his wife, and in his sudden revulsion of feeling against the "lying" Frocin whom he now means to punish, should end his monologue with a gratuitous historical footnote. To whom would it be directed? It is Béroul's general practice to end speeches strongly rather than weakly; and these four lines if read as attributed to Marc are lame and dispensable. I consequently surround them with parentheses.

285 Tristran had left the garden but not the vicinity of the palace; see 529f.

298–305 On Marc's misreading of signs, here and later in the Morrois (2001–13), see Sargent-Baur, "Truth, Half-Truth, Untruth," 396–411.

322–31 On these astronomical data, which place the scene in July before sunrise, see Henry, "Sur les vers 320–338," and Braet/Raynaud de Lage II.

326 Ewert takes this to mean "when he learned of"; Poirion and Braet/Raynaud de Lage II understand it similarly (yet the phrase seems to apply to all births throughout the kingdom). Gregory and Lacy follow the text: "when he heard," sc. a newborn's cry.

328–34 Frocin will "deceive" his master in the sense of forestalling the fate predicted by the stars. He flees towards Wales and cannot be found (337, 385), yet will soon be brought back for advice (635–9). See Ewert II, and Braet/Raynaud de Lage II, note.

352–69 Iseut's speech brims with self-congratulation on her own performance.

357–8 The imperfects imply repetition.

381 Maistre: Governal plays the role of confidant, tutor, squire, and companion-in-arms.

390 A king normally went about accompanied; see 1926–40, 2096, and 2113–15.

399 That is, since his banishment from the palace (?).

418–19 "Nothing," i.e., about his reason for sending for me (Reid).

494–504 Braet/Raynaud de Lage II note Iseut's echoing of Marc's false reasoning and language in 298–305 (which Iseut, though, had not overheard).

511–18 Brengain's tale of Tristran's enmity towards her seems gratuitous; yet it does reinforce the general theme of deception. See Béroul's comment on his character's performance, 519–22.

527 Iseut can permit herself to smile or laugh, discreetly, at Brengain's stratagem and/or the happy conclusion of her own manoeuvrings. Marc's reaction is both stronger and simpler.

528 Brengain does not need to seek Tristran at his lodgings, as ordered (507), although he has had ample time to return there from the garden (285).

529–32 Presumably the wall is the outer wall of the palace, and of the royal chamber as well; we shall see (2457–68) that the window of the latter opens to the outside (as does the rear window-slit, 4314f.). Braet/Raynaud de Lage II read these lines as an interpolation "puisque aux v. 536ss. Brangain paraît avoir rejoint Tristan chez lui, où elle lui expose une situation nouvelle pour lui. Il n'était donc pas 'à la paroi.'" Yet Béroul states that Tristan had heard both women speak with the king, and Brengain's "here in his house" (536) would fit her unexpected encounter with Tristran eavesdropping *here*, just outside the chamber and palace wall. She seemingly is unaware of what he has heard.

561 Braet/Raynaud de Lage II draw attention to the frequent (and frequently insincere) invocation of the name of God: thirty-two times from line 5 to here.

606f The barons evoke the contractual nature of feudal relations: a king rules with the consent of the land-holding magnates, who owe him counsel and military service but may withhold both if seriously offended.

614–17 The barons' accusation is that Marc is aware of the situation and condones it, thus scanting honour and duty; they will no longer tolerate this open scandal.

636 Latin: the learned language, and by extension learning in general.

650, 684 If **Carduel** is Carlisle, as most scholars think, the distance to it from Marc's residence in western Cornwall is very considerable, requiring a ride of some weeks. This length of absence presumably enters into the dwarf's calculations.

652–4, 686 The practice was to write on a piece of parchment, fold it, and seal it with wax. The recipient would break the seal and unfold the document.

657 Parler (= to speak) can suggest an amorous encounter; see 733–4 and Tobler-Lommatzsch VII, 291.

657–63 We note Frocin's rude way of referring to the queen, without name or title.

677 If containers were lacking, medieval people sometimes used a fold of their clothing for transporting small measures of meal, etc.

681 Tristran is Marc's chamberlain, and his only nightly guardian.

695 A lance-length would be some ten or twelve feet.

701f The whole episode takes place at night, but of course not in total blackness. Tristran watches Frocin sprinkling the flour, then sees him and Marc go out (722–4). There is enough (natural) light for him to leap to Iseut's bed and back again (729–46). The dwarf returns with a candle; now king and barons see the blood on the floor, the sheets, and Tristran's leg (766–77).

726 The line alerts us to the degree of midnight darkness in the chamber: it is not complete, for Tristran successfully jumps the space between the two beds.

736–7 "He sees by the moon … " He does not observe them *by* the moonlight (*pace* Payen, Gregory, Lacy, Braet/Raynaud de Lage II) but reads *in* the moon what is occurring; in 321–4 he similarly observed stars and planets, then too being out of doors. Walter and Poirion understand these lines as I do.

750–4 How Iseut, unaware of Tristran's imminent departure and of his rash plan to "speak" to her before leaving by leaping into the bed just vacated by the king, could have known of those potentially incriminating blood-stains in an ill-lit chamber (see 725–6), and how, even if she had suspected them (why should she?), she could have removed the sheets (what would she have done with them?) on the sudden return of Marc and Frocin, are not matters that trouble Béroul, who needs the stains to drive the story forward.

755–6 I take this as parenthetical: an authorial anticipation of things to come. Walter expands 756 with "par la suite" ("later"), Gregory adds "[eventually]."

771 Owing to Béroul's excitable and incremental way of presenting events, we learn only now that Marc has arrived accompanied by the three barons.

809–26 Another authorial interjection.

821–5 Béroul does not explain how Tristran, seized in his bed (hence naked and without a weapon), could have killed three (presumably armed) men. Commentators have seemingly not raised the question.

833–59 This long chorus voices the townspeople's unanimous support for Tristran, who had saved them in the place of the cowardly native barons (850–2).

873 Prime: the first of the canonical hours; about 6 a.m.

875 The **cort** is wherever the king is at the moment.

882–3 For this (anachronistic) mode of execution, see Jonin, 69–70.

899 Tristran's hands are bound; see 941.

902–8 The lovers were held in the palace. Tristran is led out first, and Iseut, having called out to him as he leaves, awaits her turn at the stake (1071).

909–11 Damledé, from **Dominus Deus**. Ezekiel 18:23: "Numquid voluntatis meae est mors impii? dicit Dominus Deus, ut non convertatur a viis suis, et vivat?" and 33:11: "Vivo ego, dicit Dominus Deus, nolo mortem impii, sed ut convertatur impius a via sua et vivat." (In the Douay version these verses read: "Is it my will that a sinner should die, saith the Lord God, and not that he should be converted from his ways, and live?" And, "As I live saith the Lord God, I desire not the death of the wicked, but that the wicked turn from his way, and live.") It seems to have escaped notice that Béroul omits the second half of each quotation – a point not without interest.

915–24 Béroul's description, beginning with **devers bise**, is unclear. Ewert and Lacy give "facing north," Gregory "faced north," Braet/ Raynaud de Lage II "face à la bise." If Béroul had the siting of the façade (= face?) in mind, this would put the chancel, altar, and window through which Tristran jumps at the opposite (south) end of the church, a most unusual alignment (and away from the cliff). Indeed, even for the chancel to be at the north, rather than east, end is not usual either. We might take the phrase as applying to the chapel as a whole, on the northernmost part of the cliff.

934f On Béroul's information about Cornish geography much has been written, a good deal of it speculative. See Padel, "The Cornish

Background" and "Beroul's Geography," and Braet/Raynaud de Lage II. Béroul claims that the Cornish still called the projecting stone **le saut Tristran** (954: "Tristran's Leap"); this hints at a toponymic tale. See Padel, "Beroul's Geography," 90.

948–61 Halfway down this dangerous cliff there juts out a large, broad stone (perhaps composed of another material). On it Tristran alights, aided by the wind (we may imagine an up-draft) that catches his clothing; from this ledge he can safely jump down to the sandy beach.

We must not make a geologist of Béroul, but he surely knew about rocks and cliffs, and he was a highly visual poet if not one given to lavishing couplets on detailed natural and geographical descriptions. This whole episode is disjointed, its focus shifting among its elements and offering some puzzling details. One might summarize: on the edge of a promontory composed of slaty stone is perched a chapel. Making its way to the pyre, Tristran's escort comes to it and allows Tristran to enter. His sole escape route is through it; out the apse window he goes. Beyond is only a cliff, dangerous even for an acrobatic animal jumping off it. But there is a wide, projecting stone. (*Pace* Padel, "Beroul's Geography," 90, the stone is not "set in a sandy beach.") Tristran drops down onto it and thence to the soft sand; then he goes bounding away (961) to freedom along the shore.

955–7 The sense is open to question, for in 874–5 we learned that all in the realm have been summoned to court (sc. to the king's presence, and just now the place where he is preparing the summary justice), and have gone there (876–9). Even the lepers have learned what is afoot, and come running to the place of execution (1155–60). One might conjecture that the summons has somehow not reached the worshippers in the nearby chapel – if indeed there are any. In the latter case, why do Tristran's guards not then and there inform them? And if the chapel is crowded with worshippers, how does Tristran manage to dash through them and past the altar to the window? To my mind, ms. 955 is a *locus desperatus*.

957 As for **Toz a genoz** (= "knees") applying not to Tristran but to the postulated worshippers, it is dubious for a reason that has not previously been advanced, to my knowledge: if any are there, why should they be kneeling (unless for private prayer or the elevation of the Host, which would imply the presence of a priest, although none is mentioned)? My conjecture is that Béroul had in mind a chapel empty yet open for private prayer; and the chance to pray is what Tristran begs of his guards (931–2).

965–74 The narration turns to the sequel of Tristran's arrest. Governal slips out of the **cité** (presumably he had, like Tristran, been staying in the palace); he has a horse, and both his own sword and Tristran's, and he flees for his life and to save his master's. (Reid's note on 204–5 is to be disregarded; no knight would leave his sword in pledge.) How Governal knows where to find Tristran is not explained – perhaps we may conjecture to a place nearby, known to be used for executions?

965–1273 All this episode is played out on two physical planes: headland and sandy shore.

973 As for "where it had remained," in the absence of any indication of where this might have been, we may suppose that the sword had remained behind in the royal chamber, where Tristran as the king's trusted guardian would have had his weapon by him (and perforce would have left it when he was seized and bound).

976–8 The masculine singular pronouns are confusing; the inversion of 977–8 makes for clarity. Tristran notices Governal at a distance; he recognizes him and hails him. Seeing his lord, Governal rejoices, and goes to him. That the mounted man should make for the one who is on foot is, I think, the more natural move.

996–7 Gregory understands: "And if she is burnt, and you do not exact swift revenge, may you never meet a young maiden in your life again!" This is psychologically unconvincing: why would Governal think that after Iseut's execution Tristran would have any interest in meeting another young girl? (NB: **ancele**, normally meaning "servant" and not "young maiden," does not appear elsewhere in Béroul or Béroul II.)

1008–9 Gregory's reading, **Trop n'os anoie** ("I am sorry to be a nuisance to you"), while possible on paleographical and syntactical grounds, is not only stilted but improbable in the cultural context. Why should a knight apologize to his squire? Of course, Tristran is weaponless, having been seized in his bed, bound, guarded, then led out to his execution. Without mentioning this detail, Reid points out the lack of reason for Tristran to say what is in the ms., mentioning that by 1903 Muret was suspicious of this half-line, and conjecturing the common Old French formula **Dex vos en oie!** ("may God hear you!") – certainly a more appropriate response to Governal's preceding speech.

1030–1 Ewert and Braet/Raynaud de Lage II print **avoé**, taken in the sense of "acknowledge as vassal" (Ewert II: "retainers"); Braet/Raynaud de Lage II give "Tous les bourgeois lui sont soumis … "

Reid suggests **soi avoer**, "acknowledge oneself as vassal." It is most unlikely that townspeople should do this; they obey the king, but as his subjects, not vassals. Gregory ("Further Notes," 11–12) retains **a voé** from **avoié** ("se mettre en route") and translates "are on your path"; but why should they be? (A general hue-and-cry is mentioned by Governal in 1036, but only as a possibility: *if* one were to be raised …)

1040 Tintagel, on the northwest coast of Cornwall, will be one of Marc's residences in 3150.

1051–4 The interpretation turns on **ont/out** (plural/singular). As Reid observes, **ont** makes better sense: Marc gave the order, the barons did the binding. One might add that the notion of the barons giving a command to the king, who carries it out (as Gregory), is implausible. As for the legal issues, and specifically the anachronistic sentence of capital punishment for adultery, see Jonin, *Personnages*, 67–70 and Ewert II.

1085 For **Dinas**, **Dinan**, and **Lidan**, see Ewert II, 145–7 (**Dinan** = personal name; **Dinas** = place-name common in Cornwall, "fortress"; **Lidan** = adjective, "large." Béroul calls the seneschal **Dinas** throughout, and makes **Dinan** his fief.)

1089–1100 Dinas first reminds Marc of his irreproachable stewardship, then proceeds to his plea for the queen; the voice of the community (1075–82) is echoed in that of a great magnate, Marc's seneschal. The king is about to lose his services for a time (see 1133–40; by 2531 he will be back at court), as well as losing the loyalty of the people generally.

1106–9 These lines have been much discussed. My interpretation is shaped primarily by Braet/Raynaud de Lage II (who oddly retain e^n **vos**, 1106). With Reid I take 1106–7 as a rhetorical question. See also Gregory, "Notes on the Text," 3–5. (His edition and translation here differ somewhat from mine.)

1119 "Give her" in the sense of entrusting her to his care. This request will be echoed in, and contrasted by, Ivain the leper's **"Yseut nos done"** ("Give Iseut to us," 1193).

1148 The only commentary on this line seems to be that of Braet/ Raynaud de Lage II, who propose that Iseut has been sewn into her gown. More probably Béroul is referring to the usual practice of sewing or lacing on the detached sleeves of a garment.

1155 Lancïen: Béroul seemingly muddles two areas: one placed by him near Tintagel, the other being Lantyan: once a manor, now a farm near Fowey. See Ewert, and Padel, "The Cornish Background," 60, 81.

The distances involved are not great (some twenty-five miles as the crow flies).

1155–65 This passage anticipates Tristran's disguise, 3297–3309, 3566–74, 3617–26, 3763–8.

1165–71 The repeated **justise** combines the notions of judgment, condemnation, and execution.

1195–7 The association of leprosy, lust, and adultery was common in the Middle Ages; see Brody, *The Disease of the Soul*, and Tristran's own account of his disease, 3761–73.

1202 As for **solaz** ("upper rooms"), it is the plural of **solier** from **solarium** (Muret, Ewert). (Cf. Middle English **sollar, soler**: a room above the great hall and thus exposed to the sunlight.) Some editors emend to **soliers**, e.g., Ewert, Payen (see his note 41), Lacy, Braet/Raynaud de Lage II. The latter signal the contrast between spacious rooms and low hovels, between the choice wines and foods to which Iseut is accustomed and the left-over bread given to the lepers. One might add that **la nostre cort** ("our court," 1211) further underscores the notion of two very dissimilar courts.

1209 We may think of the lepers as having had experience of getting scraps at the doors of Marc's residence; it is noteworthy that Tristran recognizes Ivain (1247).

1226 Here Béroul evokes two groups: the loudly grieving townspeople (1142–4) and the jubilant lepers.

1229 Ivain leads rather than carries Iseut away; see also 1247. *Pace* Braet/Raynaud de Lage II, it is most improbable that a leper, even a chief of lepers, living on scraps (1208–9) should be mounted; see note on 1259.

1245 Béroul does not narrate Governal's dismounting and Tristran's mounting while in their ambush; by now it has already happened. **Fiert** may mean "he whips" or "he spurs," but spurs are not mentioned among the pieces of equipment Governal has brought, whereas a switch can easily be improvised. Tristran sets out first, Governal follows on foot as fast as he can, 1259f.

1251–5 The removal of the outer garment is a normal preliminary to a fight (see 1981 and 4381); here, grotesquely, the weapons will be crutches.

1259–62 A knight is above attacking his inferiors, but a squire may do so (yet Governal uses a tree-branch, not his sword). Ivain, like Governal, must be on foot (the note of Braet/Raynaud de Lage II for line 1270 is in error); for a squire to strike a mounted man (even a leper), disable him, and rescue his captive is a most unlikely feat.

1264–71 Less than clear. I take it that it is Tristran who seizes the freed Iseut with his right hand (the left hand, of course, holding the reins) and helps her up onto his steed (1271). The two ride off, with Governal following on foot.

1265–70 Here Béroul rejects the version of the incident in his (and Eilhart's) source. To belittle others who have told a tale, and claim that the present account is the authentic one, is a common trope (see, e.g., the prologue to *Erec et Enide* of Chrétien de Troyes). *Vide infra* **1789–92** and note. (There is no indication that Ivain carries Iseut away on his horse, as Braet/Raynaud de Lage II, note on 1270.)

1271 Tristran goes off with the queen, he carrying her on his horse.

1275 Suddenly the three fugitives are in the Morrois forest (Moresc, west of Truro in southwest Cornwall). On this then-extensive forest, the largest in the area, see Loth, "Le Cornwall et le roman de Tristan"; also Ewert II and Padel, "The Cornish Background," 61–3.

1279–84 The bow and two arrows will become attributes of Tristran; see 4292–3 and 4422–3.

1306–50 This incident figures in no other version of Tristan's story. See Ewert II, Newstead, Padel, "The Cornish Background," 65. It amounts to an etymological jest (*marc* being Celtic for "horse"; here the anecdote may be a reminiscence of the classical tale of King Midas and his ass's ears, as related by Ovid. For the theme of a king with horse's ears, see Milin; for Béroul's treatment, see Milin, 265–6).

The whole passage, set off by **Oiez** and **Seignors**, has the air of being an hors d'œuvre. Its only contribution to the narrative is the elimination of the dwarf.

1320 The Perilous Ford is mentioned here for the first time; it is another name for the Mal Pas, still on modern maps, a marshy area bordering a tributary of the Truro River, fordable at low tide but only with difficulty. (There is also a good crossing-place, known to both Tristran and Governal; see 3590–1.) See Braet/Raynaud de Lage II, and Padel, "Beroul's Geography," 84–7.

1339–47 The barons' speech and behaviour are very curious, as are Marc's. Why he should deign to respond to their insolence, and *a fortiori* laugh or smile at it (**senrist**, 1343), then suddenly pass to violence, is not explained. Braet/Raynaud de Lage II: "ce rire est sardonique ou cruel: il prélude à la vengeance" ("This laugh is sardonic or cruel: it foreshadows vengeance"). It is true that Marc is given to brusque changes of mood (Perinis remarks on this in 3432–3), but not without motivation. Reid: "perhaps Muret's **s'iraist** ("becomes angry") should be salvaged." (The reference is to M^1 and M^2.) This suggestion is persuasive. Marc is irascible; see **irascuz** (3204), and the proposed emendation of **sitaise** to **s'iraise** in 3072.

1351–6 A break in the narrative, with recapitulation of 965–70.

1389 Ewert, glossary, at **asez**: "quite"; Reid's "as good as dead" or "might as well be dead" gives a better sense.

1391–2 The repetition of the rhyme-word in the ms. is suspect. Perhaps the first **penitance** means "penance" (to be followed by absolution).

1431–6 Another recapitulation. (Ewert takes it as an "Interpolation introduced by *Seignors* [?]"; but 1351–6, with a very similar structure, is not so characterized.) Marc's ban, of which Tristran has been informed by Ogrin in 1370–6, is here treated as new information. The **ne**ⁿ **a**ⁿ **goise** of 1434 is regularly taken by editors and translators as coming from the infinitive **angoissier**, "to cause dismay" (Ewert). (Gregory, though, identifies it as third person singular subjunctive of **angroissier**, prints Ewert's **n'en** as **nen**, and understands: "In Cornwall there is not a parish where the rumour does not grow/ swell that … " ["Further Notes," 16–17]. Yet a royal, country-wide proclamation amounts to much more than a rumour; and a general reaction to it of dismay is of a piece with Béroul's reiterated statements of Tristran's being held by the Cornish as the national saviour, and beloved.

1461–2 A reference to a widely known tale, a version of which is in the *Gesta Romanorum*, tale 124 (where these words are not Solomon's but are spoken before him; see Lecoy, "Sur les vers 1461–1462," 82–5 and Ewert II).

1468 Like Muret[4] and Reid, I take 1468–72 as an aside.

1469–72 Another of Marc's sudden shifts of mood; see note on 1339–47.

1473–4 It is not specified whether these barons are the three **felon**, as Braet/Raynaud de Lage II. Three is a conventional number.

1493–4 This must be the private lodging outside the palace, used by Tristran after his banishment from the royal chamber (see 218 and 228). In 3609–10, Governal will go to this place (?) to collect Tristran's equipment and war horse; see 3586–8.

1544 Like the human characters, the dog can shed tears; see 1452.

1563–6 Unwittingly, the tracking-dog has tracked down his master at the risk of his own life.

1587f Even the dog is drawn into the motif of concealment.

1591–2 These lines will be echoed in 4441 and 4457.

1618–19 Tristran incites the dog, which fails the test; thereupon Tristran begins his training.

1653–5 Interpretations differ; see Vinaver, "Pour le commentaire"; Ewert II; Reid, *Commentary* and *Medieval Miscellany*, 282; Braet/Raynaud de Lage II; Sandqvist; and Gregory.

1656–1721 Here Governal kills one of Tristran's three enemies, but later there will still be three of them, in the part of the romance I attribute to Béroul II.

1661–3 These lines pose a problem of sense. Given the assertion that the Cornish, every one of them, shunned the Morrois, what is that hunter doing there along with his followers? Are we to assume that they are not Cornish? Yet this important but here nameless huntsman is one of the three who had exposed the lovers (1656–7, 1719–20), and Governal will soon recognize him (1687–8) and kill him. To complicate matters, all three **felon** are named and are still alive and well in 3137–8, 3474–5, and 4237–8. (This feature has been adduced to support the hypothesis of dual authorship of the romance.)

1678f Throughout this scene the verb tenses alternate frequently and disconcertingly. The sequence of events, less than clear, seems to be: Governal hears dogs that are chasing a stag. He sees a lone rider approaching, recognizes him, and kills him when his mount stumbles (or falls). Governal goes off with the rider's head. Then come the hunters, following stag and dog-pack. Seeing the headless body, and believing that Tristran did the deed, they flee the forest and spread the news.

1686–9 This most hated enemy of Tristran is strangely not identified, here or in 1746.

1690–3 The huntsman's brutal treatment results in breakneck speed; the horse's stumbling (or falling) presumably slows its approach enough to enable Governal to strike.

1694–5 Governal, in ambush, steadies himself against a tree; see 4373.

1698–9 There is no stated reason why this enemy should suspect that Tristran is nearby.

1702 That is, burned and his ashes cast to the wind.

1735–8 The reference must be to the forked branch propping up the bivouac, and not antlers (as Gregory, here and in note on 1291). Antlers are scarcely indicated for the central support of a hut, however temporary, with plenty of branches available.

1739–44 Braet/Raynaud de Lage II place this scene in a series of increasingly threatening intrusions by the external world: first Husdent, then this **felon**, and at last Marc himself.

1740 We note again that Tristran is given to spasmodic action.

1752–60 For the history of such a device see Ewert II, Braet/Raynaud de Lage II, and Legge, "The Unerring Bow." Béroul's description of it is far from clear, as the abundance of commentaries and translations attests. None is entirely persuasive, and the difficulties may well go back to a scribal misunderstanding (or even to authorial confusion).

1763–4 These lines have generated several interpretations, none wholly satisfactory; see Ewert, Reid, Braet/Raynaud de Lage II, Gregory (edition and "Further Notes," 17–18). Unlike the latter and also Braet/Raynaud de Lage II, I think that the implied **il** ("he") of 1764 cannot refer to Tristran; the whole point of the device is that it will function in its maker's absence. Any solution to the problem must be tentative.

1774–6 Pentecost can fall over a five-week period, 10 May–13 June, depending on the date of Easter. Most translators have understood "en icel tens que l'en aoste" as referring to harvest-time; but even mid-June or slightly later is early for harvesting, though not for hay-making, as Payen's translation conveys ("à l'époque des fenaisons," p. 57).

1783–92 Another authorial aside.

1788 "Such a draught," sc. of suffering. Lines 1783–8 have been treated variously by translators.

1789–90 One more claim to the authenticity of Béroul's account (see 1265–70), with the added detail of Béroul's drawing on the written source.

1793 Tristran's return journey is not narrated; the poet skips to his arrival.

1805–6 There is no indication that the sword is intended as a chastity symbol; it is simply a normal precaution. That Marc reads it symbolically is another matter; see Sargent-Baur, "Truth, Half-Truth, Untruth," 403–11.

1807–10 Sleeping naked was usual (at least at night). That the lovers happen to be clothed – and in hot weather – is odd but providential. Braet/Raynaud de Lage II propose that they are too overcome by the heat to take the time to undress.

1838, 1840 For **fu[e]llier[s]** Reid proposes "trampled grass"; Braet/Raynaud de Lage II offer "traces, endroits piétinés" for 1838, and suggest that the word does not necessarily have the same meaning in both lines. I conjecture this scenario: the nameless forester happens upon spots where the lovers had encamped on, say, the last couple of nights, and follows their trail to where they are now.

1842 The ms. **saunee** is obscure, witness the various translations proposed. Perhaps "reunion"?

1845–1904 The actions and details in this passage are badly muddled, yet seemingly have not drawn comment. The forester's terror, flight, and speed are mentioned repeatedly. First he moves away from the sleeping lovers out of fear of Tristran (1845–9, 1894), who would kill him if he awoke; he himself could give no hostage except for his head, left in pledge (1847–8) – and for what? The narrator repeatedly stresses his speed (1845, 1850, 1856, 1862, 1867–70), as does King Marc (1871–5). The forester has another motivation for his long run (roughly five or six miles each way): desire for reward (1856–62) and respect for the king's general ban (1884–7). Anyone in the kingdom who found Tristran was to capture him or report him (1884–7), on pain of death. Yet, having brought his report, the runner dreads Marc's anger and possible summary justice (1888–9). Not only is he confident that the lovers will still be there and asleep when he returns there with the king, but he associates himself with the projected act of vengeance (**ja seron d'eus vengiez**, 1903). The following two lines, stating that if Marc does not avenge himself on them he has no right to rule, are of an amazing insolence.

Compared with these narratorial problems, the statement that the runner came down the hill (1866; none has previously been mentioned, but see 2445) and ran (unchallenged) up the steps into the hall (1868–70) is of minor importance.

1889 Braet/Raynaud de Lage II attempt to account for these misgivings: the forester fears punishment for bearing bad news. Ewert also notes this possibility.

1916 The narrator invokes the *gutta serena*, which leads to blindness – a fitting punishment for someone who has seen too much (see the death of the spying Godoïne, at the end of the preserved fragment).

1932–7 This is the flimsiest of pretexts.

1939 A mistaken reference to the *Disticha Catonis* or medieval translations thereof (Ewert).

1944–8 As Braet/Raynaud de Lage II observe, Marc had abandoned Iseut to the lepers, and Tristran had rescued her from them, before taking to the woods; yet here he mentally accuses Tristran of carrying her off. I add that once again the poet shows the king as inconsistent as well as impulsive.

1944–50, 1954–6 An interior monologue. (Marc forgets that he has cast Iseut off.)

1949 I follow Sandqvist's suggestion that the second hemistich is parenthetical.

1952 Batany (47) reads the line as meaning "détruire l'ensemble de souillures qu'il vient de se rappeler"; but killing the sinners can scarcely destroy the sins. I take the hemistich as one of many authorial interventions.

1970 A **marc** was a large monetary unit. (The rhyme suggests a pun.)

1971 I accept Reid's interpretation of **a son forfet** (as do Gregory, Braet/Raynaud de Lage II, and Lacy).

1976 He holds the off-side stirrup, as was usual, while the rider dismounts on the near side.

1978 It is tempting to make the plural **lient** of the ms. into a singular, dissyllabic **lie**. The forester is acting as the king's squire, and it would not take two men to tether a horse to the branch of a tree. After the horse is secured the two men move off together, the forester knowing just where to go.

1979–87 They have proceeded a little distance when they see the **loge**. Marc pauses, sheds his cloak, unsheathes his sword, then moves away alone from that spot (**s'en torne**), no longer needing guidance. Although his weapon is drawn, there can be no question of his brandishing it in this setting of trees and underbrush (as Gregory, who reads ms. **sentorne** as **lentorne**, translation and glossary). He advances furiously towards the **loge** and enters it.

1985–6 The interior monologue resumes briefly, as Marc moves rapidly ahead of his guide.

1987–9 Context requires the rejection of (1987) **entre** (perhaps copied from the line above, or from **soventre** in the same line): how can the forester "enter behind" the king into a small, improvised, and temporary shelter (see 1640–1) – and to what purpose? Yet most translators so understand these lines. Problematical also is the sequence: first entering the shelter, then approaching it. It is plain that Marc, having got ready for action, rapidly goes ahead without awaiting the other man who hastens after him. Marc gestures to him to turn back. (He will later rejoin him where the horse is tied, and peremptorily dismiss him, 2052–4.)

1991–2 One of the most debated couplets in the poem. Henry ("Du subjonctif d'imminence") reads **ire** and **tresva**, and makes **ire** the subject of both verbs in 1992: sc., "anger makes him do it, then passes off"; Ewert proposes (II, 186) that Mark's "strength fails him"; Lacy "he could go no farther"; Payen "il est plein de fureur, et prêt à défaillir"; Walter "sa colère l'excite puis s'apaise soudainement"; Gregory "[when, suddenly] his anger left him and vanished"; Braet/ Raynaud de Lage "La colère le lui fait faire, mais elle se dissipe." This seems too drastic a change to be compressed into the eight syllables of 1992. (It is not until 2011–12 that Marc puts away his wrath.)

1993–2001 To all such interpretations one can only say: Why should Marc's anger pass off? The blow is about to fall on both the sleeping lovers when the king notices details that give him pause (1995–2000); *then* he hesitates for four lines (2001–4), *then* he mentally reviews (2005–10) the signs of guilt he had expected to see but does not, *then* he decides not to strike after all (2011–14), and considers (2015–19) what would be the consequences if he did kill them. It must be his (mis)reading of the signs that causes him to abandon his murderous plan. I add that Marc, though given to sudden changes of mind and mood, does not do so without motivation.

2007–16 See Sargent-Baur ("Truth, Half-Truth, Untruth," 403–4, 405–10), and Braet/Raynaud de Lage II on Marc's misreading of the signs (cf. 301, closely echoed in 2007), and change of plan.

2027–31 For the ring, see 1811–13.

2032 Why Marc carries fur gloves, having set out hastily in a heat-wave (see 1794), is not explained, and has not elicited commentary. I assume that **deslié** (2039) means "untied," i.e., from his belt; Marc would scarcely be wearing them while handling his sword.

2039–50 See the lengthy note in Braet/Raynaud de Lage II on the feudal implications of the signs left by the king, which the lovers will misunderstand. Structurally the two attempts at interpretation balance each other: Marc takes as proofs of innocence the clothing and posture of the lovers (which do not, seemingly, conform to their usual practice; see 1805–25) and so abandons his plan to kill them, while Tristran and Iseut will soon read the signs deliberately left by Marc not as tokens of his clemency but as warnings of vengeance to come. See Sargent-Baur, "Truth, Half-Truth, Untruth," 405–10.

2044 I take **il** to refer to the finger, as does Ewert (as against M[4] and Reid). Gregory prints **il** but translates "she."

2053–4 There is no reference here to the reward promised in 1912–13 and in 1969–71.

2063–72 Thematically, Iseut's dream anticipates her situation in the formal exculpation; see 4185 and note.

2081 I adopt Reid's suggested punctuation. The line evokes a detail figuring in other accounts of the story, but lacking in the fragments of Béroul and Béroul II: Tristran, in battling the Morholt, struck his helmeted head and so gave him what was to prove a mortal wound. A piece of Tristran's sword, remaining in his enemy's skull, was retrieved therefrom after the corpse was returned to Ireland, and was preserved by Iseut, who later matched it to the notch in the sword of the disguised Tristran (wounded in some versions by the Morholt's poisoned spear, in others sickened by a dragon's venom). Much of this episode is recounted by Tristran himself in the *Folie de Berne*, 395–420.

2084–5 In 2044–8 Marc has removed his ring from Iseut's finger; the act of replacing it with his own (Iseut's wedding gift to him, which he has until now been wearing) is not narrated. This latter ring will return in 2707–20; see note on those lines.

2096–8 Tristran's conjecture is odd, given that it was normal for a king to be escorted at all times. See also 2111–18.

2125–9 The three fugitives will head in the direction of Wales. They will cross the Morrois by dint of several days' travel (yet by 2268–9 we learn that not only are they still in the woods but they are not very far from Ogrin's hermitage).

2133–2304 In this long exposition Béroul repeatedly drives home the potion's effects, now supplying the detail of their exact duration as intended by Iseut's mother; see 2133–64.

2147–59 That is, on the day following the Feast of St John the Baptist, which falls on 24 June. This detail serves to date the drinking of the potion on the voyage from Ireland and the beginning of the love-affair (not narrated in Béroul's fragment). The projected duration of the potion is also mentioned in 2139–40, 2162, and (enigmatically) 3760, but nowhere else with such a degree of precision; even the time of day (2156–9) is supplied here.

2205–10 A succinct reference to the plan that miscarried.

2206–10, 2217–20 Iseut both blames Brengain and exonerates her.

2217f Curiously, Tristran's return from hunting is not narrated. Iseut's monologue leads without transition into Tristran's long speech and the subsequent dialogue.

2246–7 It is not clear whether Béroul had a particular area (and king) in mind, e.g., southwestern Scotland (Dumfries?), or simply had Tristran consider offering his services to the first lord he might encounter, as his vague reference to Brittany also suggests. Tristran, suddenly freed like Iseut from the power of the love-potion, begins to envisage their separation and contemplate his departure for a destination that is still vague. He will again mention a possible self-imposed exile, to **Bretaigne** or **Loenois**, when consulting Ogrin, 2309–10, and will raise the prospect of going off to serve the **roi de Frise** in his letter to Marc, 2610.

We note that all areas mentioned in the poem are Celtic lands (if **Frise** = Dumfries).

2259–60 Braet/Raynaud de Lage II point to Béroul's inconsistency. The potion shared on the crossing from Ireland is responsible for the disastrous passion of the lovers, here as also in 1384 and 1413–15; yet their love will be prolonged after the three-year term of the philtre.

2268 Ms.: **tornastes** (second person plural); the allusion is to 1362f., where they had happened upon Ogrin's hermitage and asked his advice. He then preached to them both at length, with an abundance of plural pronouns, 1393f. It seems that only Jonin has accepted **tornasmes** (first person plural) and translated accordingly (p. 107 and note 20).

2268–9 Although it took the lovers several days on foot to reach the area where they have been hiding (see note on 2125–9), Ogrin's hermitage is, to Iseut's knowledge, at the edge of the wood they are in.

2270–84 See the perceptive remarks of Braet/Raynaud de Lage II.

2280–4 The lovers, rather than having fled as far as Wales, are still near enough to the hermitage (presumably in the Morrois) to reach it fairly soon, and contemplate with Ogrin's help sending a message to the king on the next day if not that very night.

2290f See the commentary of Braet/Raynaud de Lage II, influenced by Le Gentil. The latter's explication of the moral and theological situation is well informed and illuminating. His analogy with the papal intervention after the flight of Lancelot and Guenièvre to the Joyeuse Garde in the *Mort Artu*, though, is of questionable relevance, since the *Mort Artu* is posterior to the *Roman de Tristran* by roughly half a century.

2307–13 See 162. This time it would be up to Marc to take the initiative.

2327–8 Iseut carefully distinguishes between two kinds of love.

2353–4 There is more than one way to understand **par bel**; Greimas gives the general sense "habilement" (cleverly); Ewert, glossary, offers "fittingly"; Jonin gives "légèrement et habilement"; Braet/Raynaud de Lage understand "à bon escient" (so also in Walter, tr.); Gregory translates "tell a white lie"; Lacy proposes "you have to be able to tell a few lies." Braet/Raynaud de Lage do well to point out (II, 104) that the lie being contemplated is a sin of omission but not of commission.

2357 That is, "I shall take a piece sufficient for a letter."

2359 Lancïen in this part of the poem is a city and royal residence. See note on 1155.

2361–2410 A passage comprising the proposed message to Marc interspersed with asides to Tristran (e.g., 2370–96). Even without Tristran's codicil, this makes for a very long letter (2429–30 confusingly aver that *all* of it is in the **brief**). The letter as subsequently read to Marc (2553–2620) corresponds in the main to 2362–2424, but with numerous differences.

2383–4 God still favours Tristran, in Ogrin's view. See 960.

2386 Costentin: presumably the modern hamlet of Constantine in Cornwall (an identification proposed by Loth, "Le Cornwall et le roman de Tristan," 83–4); but it may be a familiar hyperbolic formula; cf. 2232 and 3410.

2408 Ms.: **depise**. If **pise** = **Frise** = Dumfries, then the **mer de Frise** must be the Solway Firth (assuming that Béroul knew something about Scottish geography), and surely not the Firth of Forth, as Muret, Ewert, and Braet/Raynaud de Lage II. Lacy: "you will cross the sea to Dumfries."

2417–20 Marc's response is to be hung at the Red Cross, perhaps by its tag (conjecture of Braet/Raynaud de Lage II). (As to the posting of the answer, see 2646–50.)

2431–2 For seal-rings with incised stones, see note on 2708.

2441f Tristran's nocturnal journey with Governal will take them from the hermitage to Lantyan and back to the hermitage. Clearly **oscur** is a relative term here, as it will be in 4352.

2449 There is no mention of Governal's being mounted; during all of the forest exile they have had but one horse between them. If Tristran rides while Governal is on foot, their travel will perforce be slow.

2455–77 The action is far from easy to conceptualize. Do the watchmen (**gaites** is feminine plural) sound their horns to announce the arrival of a stranger after dark (Braet/Raynaud de Lage II), or simply because this is the normal practice at the close of day? (See the corresponding signal on the Blanche Lande at dawn on the day of Iseut's *escondit*, 4116.)

As for Tristran's movements, they too are less than clear. He enters the town, goes down into the moat (presumably the moat of the royal residence) or else follows it downhill, and soon comes up to the hall of the palace. He does not enter it (the **en** of 2458 is misleading) but approaches the window in the outside wall. Here he is able to call softly to the sleeping king, awaken him, speak with him briefly, and place his letter on the windowsill. Then he hastens away (not by the town gate?) and rejoins Governal.

2483 That is, they enter the enclosure around the structure(s); Tristran arrives on his horse (and oddly does not dismount until 2508).

2531 Dinas has by now returned to court, having left it in 1139–40.

2556–62 An allusion to another episode not in Béroul but in other versions of the tale.

2558 Ms.: **horlande**. M⁰, glossary, suggests **Norlande**. M² emends to "en demande" (?). M⁴, glossary, gives "nom de lieu inconnu"; Ewert, index: "scribal error for Irlande"(?). Most modern editors print **Irlande**, making the place-name rhyme with itself. Gregory keeps **Horlande** and translates "Ireland." I venture the paleographically distant "en cele lande."

2565–80 This section of Béroul's poem with its exchange of letters, as edited and explicated here, is a composite of my tentative solutions to its numerous challenges, with which a good many scholars have wrestled. The diplomatic transcription of the ms. in the Critical Edition volume may be useful in illustrating the problems of interpretation involved.

2575–2603 This central part of Tristran's dictated letter swings between the prospect of future burning and his memory of the past danger of it. At court he has only enemies.

2585–6 The **aventure** was no chance happening; Tristran attributes Iseut's escape from being wrongfully executed to God's pity and justice (which, by implication, aided his own exploits).

2610–12 For the **roi de Frise** (seemingly associated by the barons with the **roi … en Gavoie**, 2631), see note on 2246–7. If **Frise** designates Dumfries, the separating **mer** (here and in 2630) must be the Solway Firth. Like Reid, I reverse the order 2611–12.

2620 One notes that there is no mention here of the **Croiz Roge**, specified in Tristran's dictated codicil (2419–20). Yet Marc directs his chaplain to hang his reply on that cross (2646, 2650).

2625–38 A unanimous chorus. The **ce** of 2627 must be comprehensive: "all this."

2631 Ms: **gavoie**; perhaps a reference to the Galloway region, near Dumfries; see note on 2246.

2633 The glossaries of Muret and Ewert give "rester"/"remain" for **soi contenir**; but see Reid ("acquit himself") and Braet/Raynaud de Lage II ("se conduire").

2640–8 That very night Marc's reply is dictated, then hung by the chaplain on the Red Cross (implying that the cross is not very far from Lantyan). Tristran's ride to fetch it (2651–6) is not narrated, but seemingly is shorter than that of the preceding night; before midnight he has obtained the letter and fetched it back to Ogrin. (This time there is no mention of his being accompanied by Governal.)

2653f La Blanche Lande ("The White Moor"): a heath in Cornwall (and a medieval manor). See Padel, "The Cornish Background," 60 and "Beroul's Geography," 88.

2662 No date was mentioned earlier (see 2638).

2675–8 Here is the missing day of restoration; the place has also not been named until now.

2695–2732 The parting of the lovers, marked by the exchange of gifts and sealed with a kiss, is patterned on the feudal rite of homage (seizin).

2704 Presumably the Law given on Mount Sinai.

2707–20 A passage comprising plans for eventualities (not included in the fragment). For Iseut's ring, which Tristran is to wear henceforth and send with his messages, see below.

2708 It is instructive to look at seal-rings. There is no need to conjecture that the jasper somehow accompanies the seal (Walter, Lacy); it is far more likely that Béroul had in mind a stone that, incised in the usual way, composed the seal itself. See 2431–2, where Ogrin takes a ring and seals his letter with a **pierre** *Pace* Braet/Raynaud de Lage II, this cannot be Iseut's wedding gift from Marc, set with emeralds or an emerald, which he had taken from her finger in the Morrois (see 1812–13 and 2028–9), for she no longer has it. It is the ring that *she* had given *him* (2084–6), the one that he had clandestinely returned to her in exchange for *his* earlier gift to *her*. Thus it is Marc's own seal-ring, Iseut's original gift, that will serve to authenticate her future messages to Tristran.

This episode is much less than clear; and the green jasper and the emerald(s) (1813, 2028) add to the confusion. I take it that only two rings are involved, those bestowed at the royal wedding and later exchanged (by Marc) in the Morrois. Presumably Iseut, having awakened and recognized her own gift to Marc, did not afterwards wear the ring: why should she? If she concealed it, this would account for her description of it to Tristran, 2707–8; if she had worn it, the description would be otiose. It is unlikely that she would have possessed *two* rings (and one a seal-ring), as a fugitive from royal justice (she was to have been burned at the stake wearing her wedding-ring, which she continued to wear until the king took it back). And if she, improbably, had had a spare, where would she have kept it under her ragged clothing (1647)? Braet/Raynaud de Lage II attempt to make sense of the obscurities here, but unconvincingly: in their view, what Iseut gives Tristran to use as a sign to her after their separation cannot be Marc's returned ring, "l'anneau que Marc a passé en échange au doigt d'Iseut, celui-ci serait trop facilement identifié; il s'agit plutôt de la bague qu'il lui a donnée (1813)." Yet Iseut's projected messages to Tristran after their separation (none is in fact sent in the preserved fragment of the poem), whether accompanied by one ring or the other, would be meant only for the eyes of Iseut's unnamed messenger (2713), and for Tristran.

2712 Here **mesage** has the usual meaning of "messenger"; see 2719–20 and 3275. (In 3405 and 3409, however the reference is to an oral message.)

2726f For the language and rites of love, see Braet/Raynaud de Lage II; for **saisine** (2732), see also 2362.

2733 The **mont** with its definite article suggests that listeners would catch the allusion (perhaps to St Michael's Mount, off the Cornish coast).

2741–4 How, when, where, and by whom these textiles and furs are converted into garments (2880–7) seems not to interest the poet.

2755 This line may mark the transition from Béroul to Béroul II; see Preface.

2759–62 In spite of this prediction, the forester will be alive and participate in the joust at the Blanche Lande, and be killed by Governal's lance (4045–52). Such discrepancies have been taken as supporting the hypothesis of dual authorship. For **gibet** (2762), Ewert's glossary gives "sling," accepted by Bromiley ("A Note on Béroul's Foresters," 39) and most translators; but this has been queried by Reid, who proposes "club" (adopted by Gregory), a far more practical weapon in a forest. Poirion gives "bâton" ("stick").

2806–8 Some editors (e.g. M⁰–M³, M⁴, Ewert, Braet/Raynaud de Lage II, Poirion, and also Sandqvist in Notes) take these lines as spoken by Iseut – Tristran – Iseut. I find this less natural than attributing the whole speech to Iseut (as do Lacy and Gregory).

2820–1 Braet/Raynaud de Lage II draw attention to the contrast between the earlier depiction of the harsh forest life and this recall of the comfortable sojourns in Orri's cellar.

2822–8 I take this as a parenthetical remark on Iseut's part. She is certain of what awaits the bodies of their enemies, and expects that their souls will be damned.

2822–36 This passage, one of the most incoherent in the poem, has generated much speculation regarding the sequence of the lines, possible lacunae, etc. See the copious notes in Reid, Braet/Raynaud de Lage II, Lacy, and Gregory ("Further Notes," 134). In this translation I print the passage with my own proposed ordering (as well as the ms. line-ordering in parentheses).

2833–4 Iseut takes for granted that Governal will accompany Tristran in his pretended exile, and will thus like his lord be kept informed by Perinis of developments at court.

2833–6 Most editors have assumed a lacuna after 2836. Gregory has made a good case for inverting two couplets: ms. 2835–6 and 2833–4. I go one step further and invert lines 2833 and 2834 themselves, thus making a direct link with 2837.

2848–9 As Iseut's escort, Tristran rides on her left and holds the rein of her palfrey with his right hand. Béroul had no need to spell out this arrangement, an entirely normal one for his contemporary audience: Tristran has Iseut on his right, facing him on her side-saddle. This of course facilitates their protracted parting conversation (2770–2842) and their embrace. See note on 4075, where Arthur will escort Iseut to her *escondit*.

2864 Defeat in a judicial duel would be a clear sign of guilt.

2868 On **Loenois** see note on 2246–7 and 2310.

2869–70 Andrez is surely not a nephew of Marc; only Tristran has been so identified hitherto, and this figure is not called Marc's nephew either before or after these lines. (And why should Marc have a nephew born at distant Lincoln, well out of Celtic territory? See the note on 2246–7.) The **le** of 2875 must refer to him, not Tristran. A knight with the same name (perhaps a character drawn from another source) will appear in 3783, 3877, and 4035, and be brought down by Tristran in 4041–4. (This is curious, but there are also two different characters both named Ivain in the poem.) See Ewert's substantial note.

2871–2 These few words of Andret will be countered by the longer chorus of the three barons, 2893–2906.

2872f One could argue for the emendation, proposed in M¹ and M² only, of **le** to **se** ("him," "himself") in 2875 (see the very similar construction in 2892, 3621, 3673, and 4137). The sequence would thus be:

Andret briefly pleads with Marc to retain Tristran in his service; Marc, moved, is close to acquiescing (2873–4); he draws him aside (clearly without Tristran) to reflect (2875); the three felons seize this opportunity to approach the king and give him contrary advice (2893–2906), which he opts to follow (2907–8). This the felons promptly report back to the assembly.

2879–89 A passage comprising simultaneous and interlocking episodes.

2893–2906 The three barons, illogically, recommend that Tristran be exiled for a year; if Iseut is faithful to Marc during this period, Tristran is to be recalled – as if Iseut had been suspected of being *generally* untrue to her husband. The device does serve to furnish the lovers with another separation, punctuated by messages, while the barons' demand for a formal self-exculpation on the queen's part creates a bridge to the dramatic *escondit* before Arthur and his knights.

2925–6 I adopt Reid's interpretation (as does Gregory): this **roi riche** must be the same one referred to in 2631–2. Like Muret, Holden, Reid, and Gregory, I emend the banal **agrant ioie** ("with great joy") to **en Gavoie**. As for **riche**, the Old French word denotes "wealthy" as well as "powerful" (kings tended to be both). Tristran here spurns Marc's offer of unlimited gold, silver, and furs; he intends to enter the service of another king, and a rich one at that. (This is presumably the same ruler across the **mer de Frise**, mentioned in Ogrin's letter, 2408–9; in their response, the assembled barons had then advised Marc that Tristran should go **au riche roi … en Gavoie / a qui li roiz escoz gerroie** [2631–2]).

2933–46 Marc and most of his barons turn back. Dinas, tarrying, comes to an understanding with Tristran (2941–6); communication is foreseen (and this implies that Tristran will not after all leave the country).

2941 A reminder of the presence of Governal, who accompanies Tristran throughout this episode of pretended departure towards the sea and exile.

2948–50 How and why Dinas is to keep Iseut with him after her reunion with Marc is not explained; there may well be a gap in the text.

2971 The street is strewn with reeds or flowers.

2973 St Samson, Golant; Lantyan is in its parish. See Padel, "The Cornish Background," 60.

2974–95 See Braet/Raynaud de Lage II on Iseut's complete acceptance into society by both people and Church.

2985 Here a **garnement** is not a ready-made article of apparel (*pace* Ewert, Jonin, Lacy, Gregory, Walter) but an adornment of some sort

(Payen: "tissu"; Braet/Raynaud de Lage: "parure"), often but not always made of cloth. Here the context shows it to be a length of costly fabric, suitable for being put to ecclesiastical use (see 2991f.).

3016f Tristran's horse disappears from the narrative, not to be mentioned again until 3587. We may imagine it, along with lance and shield, as hidden somewhere (in the souterrain?) until needed; see 3586–8.

3021 The planted hedges were used as traps for large game.

3041–9 An unusually convoluted statement, perhaps expressive of the barons' muddled thinking. Lines 3042–3 might be understood: "If the queen is rumoured to be unchaste, she has never cleared herself (and this is said to your shame)."

3045 Braet/Raynaud de Lage II draw attention to the felons' claim to speak for all the barons, whereas in 2624–38 they all had urged Marc to take Iseut back.

3056f It is not easy to make sense of Marc's outbursts, 3056–79, 3082–6, 3104–8 (if this last is not an internal monologue), and 3125–36. Tristran has been gone for less than a month (3031), to serve the **roi riche** (2926) and to be recalled after a year's absence if Iseut behaves herself (2901–5). (How could she not, in Tristran's absence?) Now the king, angry with the three barons, threatens to bring Tristran from wherever he may be **hors du pays** (3065) and with amazing speed, indeed on the next day (3078–79), and soon reaffirms his intention to recall him (3085–6).

Béroul II depicts a man made irrational by the endless repetition of what he had never desired to hear. His wrath makes him imprudent to the point of riding back unescorted to Tintagel (3148–52), where he announces to Iseut his expectation of Tristran's imminent return (3197), although Tristran has not yet been summoned.

3077 A **jeu parti** is normally a choice between two (frequently undesirable) possibilities, but here it is more of a wager, indeed a threat.

3080–6 We must imagine the barons, intimidated, riding away while Marc shouts after them.

3099–3100 The barons resolve never again to speak of Tristran to Marc; and in fact they do not.

3104–8 Lines 3104–5 suggest an interior monologue (see 3165); yet 3106–8 seem to imply that the three men have heard the king's threat.

3115–16 The ms. gives these lines in inverse order; correction of Muret, accepted by Reid and adopted by Braet/Raynaud de Lage, Lacy, and Gregory. That **cil** (3115) refers to Tristran, who has already departed for a year's exile, is very unlikely (*pace* Ewert, Reid, and

Braet/Raynaud de Lage II); it is more probably a general statement, as Gregory holds (contrasting a hypothetical enemy with their real and loyal selves).

3120 A rare Béroulian joke.

3129–30 These lines have generated various interpretations. In 3129 is the mood indicative or imperative? And what does **a terre pié** (not attested elsewhere, according to Reid) signify? Could it be a scribal error for **a terre, a pié**? The three felons had dismounted for their private conference on the heath: **en la lande sor un jarri / sont decendu tuit troi a pié** (3088–9). Can they have gone back to the king and addressed him on foot, as Braet/Raynaud de Lage II and Gregory? Surely not. From the **lande** to the **chanp** there must be a little distance, and it would be abnormal for knights to walk if they could ride (hence I take **alez** to be imperative, leading into 3130). Poirion's version of 3129 as "Votre argument ne tient pas debout" ("Your argument does not hold up") does not hold up.

3132–3 Legge's identificaton of the **mer** with the Firth of Forth is persuasive; see "Place-Names and the Date of Beroul," 171–4.

3137 A suspect line (the three barons are already before Marc, 3102). This may be a narrative break, or a brief recapitulation of 3101–36.

3137–9 Here the felons are named for the first time. On their motivation, and the history of their names, there are shrewd observations in Ewert and Braet/Raynaud de Lage II.

3143–7 The theme of the barons' revolt reappears now with authorial comment; see Braet/Raynaud de Lage II.

3150 On Tintagel as a residence of King Marc, see Ditmas, "The Invention of Tintagel," 131–6.

3152–62 Marc's appearing alone would be abnormal (see 1926–8 and note on 390), yet he has departed in angry haste from his second interview with the barons (3142), without staying for any dog or huntsman (3149), arrives at the castle unannounced, and bursts, sword girded and unaccompanied (3162), into the royal chambers. It is another illustration of Marc's tendency to act impetuously, and alarmingly.

3163–4 This is clearly an internal monologue, as 3165 attests.

3166–70 Again, Béroul attends to physiological signs.

3190 Ewert II: "the felons will nevermore fear my hostility"; Reid suggests that they "have no longer any need to fear my hostility."

3193 Another example of the king's self-deception.

3197 This is wishful thinking, for Tristran was to absent himself from Cornwall for a year (2902), and has been gone less than a month

(3031). But Marc speaks more truly than he knows, for Tristran, in hiding nearby, will indeed soon return (in disguise) for Iseut's oath at the Mal Pas.

3203–7 Again, the narrator reports the unvoiced thoughts of the character.

3210–76 We now witness a bravura performance on Iseut's part, its cleverness underscored by the **sinplement** of 3209 (naïvely? humbly?). Iseut is all helplessness, injured innocence, and dependence on Marc for advice. She proceeds to sketch out an elaborate plan of action.

3211 Reid terms this a proverbial expression.

3226–7 Marc seemingly thinks that the banished felons (3131) are still nearby, since he proposes that Iseut make her **escondit** (formal denial) that very day (3226). He is being impetuous, as usual, and seems to have in mind a quick and *pro forma* disclaimer.

3228–72 The observations of Braet/Raynaud de Lage II on Iseut's taking charge are very much worth noting, as are Jonin's in *Personnages*, 81–8.

3228–76 Iseut's detailed plan is cunningly introduced by a request for Marc's advice (3229); but at the end he merely approves of it – in three words.

3239–64 Iseut asserts that, although without kin nearby, she is not friendless; she counts on King Arthur and his household knights acting in place of blood-relatives. Here for the first time Arthur is introduced into this romance.

3242–3 Interpretations differ. I take these lines as referring not to her lack of family in Cornwall (who might lead a war or revolt, as Ewert and Walter), but to what she is about to propose.

3244–76 Noteworthy are the speed and detail with which Iseut conceives her **escondit**: specific witnesses and guarantors, the presence of Arthur and his three greatest supporters and a hundred such vassals (as well as all Marc's subjects, rich and poor, on pain of being disinherited), the site of the event, the sending of the messenger to King Arthur.

3268 On the geography evoked see Padel, "Beroul's Geography," 88.

3275 Here **message** means "messenger" (*pace* Payen, Walter, Lacy, and Gregory; see Ewert's glossary). (Braet/Raynaud de Lage translate 3274–5 as "dès que le roi Arthur / aura mon message" ["as soon as King Arthur / will have my message"], but the ms. reads **verra** [will see].) Arthur will not *see* a message; Iseut in fact will send him only an oral communication, to be delivered by Perinis; see 3412f. (We may assume that Arthur, like Marc [2510f.], cannot read.) Iseut's message to Tristran, to be conveyed by Perinis, will also be oral; see 3294–3314 and 3327–8. (In 3405 and 3409, **mesage** will denote "communication.")

3291 The line implies that Iseut will inform Tristran of what she has suffered this year; but their separation has lasted less than a month (3031), and Tristran has had news through Perinis before this. Again, the chronology is elastic. The feminine singular past participle applies, ungrammatically, to both **peine** and **ahan**, 3290.

3294–3312 Iseut's message to Tristran specifies where he is to be, and his disguise and behaviour as well; it reveals nothing of her own plans (and so creates suspense for the audience). As for the place and date fixed for the **escondit**, everyone in the country somehow is informed (3283–4).

3294–6 This anticipates Iseut's crossing of the ford, 3896f.

3298 On the Mal Pas ("Bad Passage") and the Lande Blanche/Blanche Lande ("White Moor"), see Loth, "Le Cornwall et le roman de Tristan," and Padel, "The Cornish Background" and "Beroul's Geography." One should note that the Mal Pas, still on modern maps, is not an isolated marsh but an area of mud-flats bordering a tributary of the Truro River. This last feeds into the Carrick Roads estuary, hence the crossing is tidal but even now fordable at low tide; see Padel, "Beroul's Geography," 86. The relation of the two sites evoked by Béroul (with the Blanche Lande not very far to the west of the Mal Pas) is accurate.

3300–2 The prescribed equipment is less than clear. On **botele/bocele**, see Reid.

3306 However Tristran is to disfigure his face, it must be with something easy to carry about, apply, and remove. "Sores" would be more feasible than "bumps" or "tumours," *pace* Ewert; some touches of red colouring-matter, e.g., blood, would suffice. See also 3716, 3763.

3307 Perhaps this posture is meant to hide his face? Later he will keep his head down (3640, 3953).

3311–12 Iseut seems to anticipate gloating over Tristran's takings.

3315 Perinis leaves the queen at Tintagel (3150–3315), but will return to her at the mysterious Lidan (3562), "the place he had come from" (3558); but no remove of the court to Lidan is narrated. This discrepancy seems to have escaped notice. (The poet may simply have reached for a rhyme-word in **–an**.)

3320 Presumably the plural designates Tristran and Governal.

3326–7 An anticipation of 3357–63.

3328 A puzzling line; it appears to have drawn no comment.

3329 Reid: "swears by all (the saints) he can think of."

3352 Almost all editors have taken **perrin** as referring to stone; the exception is Gregory, who understands it as the oblique (and unique) form of Perinis; but the name is elsewhere invariable and always spelled with one **r**. Why Tristran should here address him by an abbreviated name, and nearly at the end of his speech, is not apparent.

3354 Ms.: **Qe l na sormoi boces menuz**: a much-discussed line. Ewert postulates a scribal confusion (**mai** for **moi**) and consequent scribal emendation of *botons to **boces**; yet this does not resolve the lack of agreement of **boces** and **menuz**. Reid gives a long note to the problem, and advances the possibility of the noun as referring to tumours on Tristran's face (see 3306 and my note on this line; see also Gregory's substantial note). No one, as far as I know, has observed that if some facial disfigurement is involved (as Iseut has specified in her message), it is odd that Tristran should use the present rather than the future tense, and especially following several futures (3334–49): he is not at this moment disfigured; why should Perinis so report him? For the poet to use such an allusion in the context of a lover's greeting is, to say the least, inept. Lacy's objection that "buds on a hawthorn" is not stylistically characteristic of Béroul is well taken, but not necessarily conclusive. I opt for the hawthorn (may-tree), and its buds or, more likely, fruit, it being midsummer.

3365 A reprise of 3356.

3365–3563 There is a phantasmagorical quality about this episode; it raises many questions. Why does Perinis seek for Arthur at Caerleon? Why, once there, must he inquire repeatedly before learning that the king is at **Isneldone**? Why, before getting there, does he ask a shepherd where the king is? How can this shepherd be informed about the domestic arrangements in the king's residence, and about the Round Table? Why does this character assure Perinis that he will indeed see the Round Table?

3373 On Isneldone, see Ewert and Reid. The identification with Snowdon in northwest Wales, rather than Stirling, appears likely, given that Perinis implausibly has a mere fortnight (3279) for the round trip to King Arthur. He first makes a detour to Tristran's refuge with Orri, then seeks Arthur in vain at Caerleon, but learning the good news (3372–3) that the king is at Isneldone, he rides on and finds him there. By the time Perinis reaches him, only a week remains (3447). After Arthur receives Iseut's messenger and hears the counsel of his great barons, he must organize his expedition and arrive at the Blanche Lande within the term announced, as indeed he does. Here Béroul II's notions of Cornish and Welsh geography seem highly vague; he has all this quest take place within a constricted and featureless area.

3379–80 The turning Round Table remains problematical; see Baumgartner, 355 and Braet/Raynaud de Lage II.

3395–3401 In the hall there is a dais, upon which Arthur and his household are seated at tables (one notes the plural). No Round Table is mentioned.

3398f Braet/Raynaud de Lage II draw attention to the new and more courtly tone here, used by Perinis and subsequently characterizing Arthur and his circle.

3407 Arthur promises to grant whatever Perinis will ask on Iseut's behalf even before the request is specified: the "rash boon" motif.

3410 Tudele (Tudela in Spain) stands for some faraway place.

3414 Foulet ("Sire, Messire (I)," 29) places the use of **mes sire Gauvain[s]** as dating after the *Chevalier de la Charrete* and the *Conte du Graal* of Chrétien de Troyes. This suggests that the latter part of the poem may have been composed, or revised, sometime in the last quarter of the twelfth century (NB, always assuming that Béroul II had access to those romances).

3423–4 Perinis echoes Marc's reproach to the barons, 3063–4.

3426–7 Ms.: fra^{n}c^{ier}; most editors emend to **François** (Frenchmen). The lines as they stand are absurd; there is no reason why there should be French or Saxon nobles at Marc's court. Furthermore, all Iseut's lineage must be Irish.

3428–9 A proverb; see Morawski #2263.

3453 Perinis has not mentioned this detail. Here the tense is present: "is leaving."

3459–94 Gawain, Girflet, and Evains appear well informed of the intrigues at Marc's court.

3461 Left unexplained is how Gawain knows who has raised this issue; see also 4237–9.

3462–70 Gawain's enmity for Ganelon is also not accounted for, but the name of the arch-traitor to Charlemagne must have been widely known by Béroul's time.

3466 Richier, another Norman saint (see note on 238).

3466–94 These threats of one king's vassals against those of another appear overwrought, absent any account of their motives.

3478–9 The difficulty of these lines is reflected in the diverse translations. With **pasent** (= pierce), the subject **li coutel** (= the blades) must be plural; but how can a lance have more than one blade or point (Ewert, note and glossary)? And how can a lance (normally round) have edges (Reid)? Furthermore, an indirect object is needed. (The only other occurrence of **coutel**, masculine singular oblique, is in 4324, clearly with the meaning "knife.")

I emend to: **Ne li passe outre le coutel** ... , understanding an implied **je** as the subject, and taking **le coutel** (usually spelled **cotel**) as denoting the coat of mail (**cotte d'armes,** the normal body-armour of a knight in joust or serious combat). Clearly Girflet has the possibility of combat in mind, although a tourney has just been evoked not by him but by Gawain and only retrospectively (3465). Furthermore, between the knights of Arthur and those of Marc any combat would perforce not be mortal, at least not by intention; Gawain had not killed Ganelon earlier but only in the course of a tourney thrust him into a mire; he is still active at Marc's court. Arthur proposes another such contest, this one in honour of Iseut (3513–14). It is most improbable that Béroul II has Girflet plotting to take revenge on Godoïne in so unsportsmanlike a manner as to use an iron-tipped lance, and before two royal courts, as editors have understood.

Hence: Girflet means to joust with Godoïne if possible and, God helping, penetrate his coat of mail with his own blunt lance. This boast is reinforced with the wish that, if he fails to realize his plan, he may never (again?) have a secret amorous encounter. If this reading is correct, it adds additional spice to 3479–80: the allusion is to two sorts of body-covering linked by the rhyme **coutel : mantel**.

3499–3503 The analogy with Iseut's case is only approximate; but see Gregory and Braet/Raynaud de Lage II (the latter observing that Iseut's recourse to Arthur is a reflection on Marc).

3504 Arthur, too, shows emotion by flushing.

3509f The king exhorts his household to put on a good show, and announces the tourney to come as being in honour of Iseut. *Pace* Padel, "Beroul's Geography," 89, the two parties do not go to the Blanche Lande "in order to hold the tournament at which Iseult swore her oath." The tournament is an hors-d'œuvre; what brings the two royal parties together is the oath-taking, which occurs on the following day.

3513 Here begins the theme of the **bohort**, a knightly sporting event with blunted lances. See the note on 3984 of Braet/Raynaud de Lage II.

3515 Ms.: **sanie amer.** All editors print **sa vie**; but there seems little question of a risk to the life of anyone reluctant to join the joust before Iseut, especially if blunt lances are to be used. (See Braet/Raynaud de Lage II, notes on 3513 and 3984.) I propose **s'amie**: displaying prowess before the queen will be a tribute to the beloved of any knight. (We note that many a knight in Arthur's train has brought with him his

drue [sweetheart, 4086], and every Cornish knight has his **feme** [wife, 4124] with him.)

3544–5 These lines are difficult, and the following allusion to spear-throwing does not much illuminate them. Ewert II (who cites a similar episode in Eilhart) translates 3545 "she will have cause to favour me greatly," but how a queen is to favour a king not her husband is open to question. Reid has reservations about the interpretations of both Muret and Ewert. Braet/Raynaud de Lage translate "Pour elle, je serai plein de zèle; / elle pourra accroître grandement mon mérite." (Again, how this might be done is not clear.) Gregory's understanding ("Further Notes," 2–3) is bold but attractive: "I will not delay [this time], because she once managed to be well ahead of me." In light of the earlier episode hinted at, and given that Arthur does indeed arrive at the Mal Pas before Iseut (he at 3702, she at 3824), we may well think that he means his eagerness to be expressed in speed.

3558–62 They are now both at Lidan, yet Perinis had departed from Tintagel; see note on 3315.

3562 Lidan is hard to localize. Braet/Raynaud de Lage II place it, oddly, in Devonshire. It seems to be the fief of Marc's seneschal Dinas (see note on 1085). If Béroul takes it to be near Tintagel, the geographical problem disappears. 4301 also implies that Dinas's residence is nearby.

One should note that the area evoked is fairly small; from Tintagel to Lantyan and from Lantyan to the Mal Pas is roughly twenty-five miles in a straight line.

3563 The significance of this datum is not apparent.

3578 It must be *with* Governal (as in Ewert, Walter, Braet/Raynaud de Lage II, and Lacy; Payen is ambiguous and Gregory gives "to"). The **maistre** is only intermittently separated from his lord; his presence has been implied throughout Tristran's "exile" and he is *au courant* with the plan. They remain together until 3606.

3582 The line has been much discussed and variously emended. Gregory comments: "Governal is referring to the fact that Yseut will take the initiative at the Malpas, in preparation for her ambiguous oath, and warning Tristran not to take any steps until indicated to do so by Yseut." Yet there is no way that Governal can know in advance of this initiative; and in fact when the lovers are both at the Mal Pas (3824f.), Iseut will give no sign to Tristran (although she will wink at Dinas, 3874). Her only communication with the "leper" will be a peremptory summons (3913f.).

3586–9 Béroul implies that Tristran's shield, lance, and steed, and those of Governal as well, have been kept nearby (in the *celier*?) during their sojourn with Orri.

3588 I take **enreigné** as encompassing the horse's usual trappings, as in 3988, to which will be added a covering, 3593–6. (Béroul will return to this; see 3999–4002.)

3602 The suggested correction of ms. **I** to **G'i** of Reid and Henry ("Pour le commentaire," 65) has weight. I add that this line, as emended, offers a contrast: "Those knights coming with Arthur will joust to win fame; I, too, shall join in."

3607–8 In the ms. these lines come between 3574 and 3576; all editors adopt Muret's correction.

3608 One would expect the squire to take leave of his master, not the other way round.

3609–10 Governal returns alone to where he and Tristran have been staying, at Orri's dwelling, then moves off with two sets of arms (his and Tristran's) and their two horses, riding one and leading the other. (Later they will both be armed and mounted for jousting, 3987f.) I take **son hernois** as covering all the equipment he is to take away to the rendezvous near the Mal Pas.

3616 Ewert's translation of the second hemistich.

3624, 3626 Here **boçuz** and **bocelé** are clearly distinguished in sense. There is no indication that Tristran ever plays the part of a hunchback. See note on 1162 in Braet/Raynaud de Lage II. In 3626 some kind of make-up is implied.

3625f The first arrivals seem to be a miscellaneous crowd preceding the two kings and their entourages and attracted, perhaps, by early rumours of the event to come.

3632 The meaning is "draw from," not "take out" (as Gregory, Lacy, and Walter). Braet/Raynaud de Lage and Poirion give "fait tirer leur(s) bourse(s)." Alms-purses were not worn under clothing but suspended from a belt, and thus were readily accessible.

3638 Since Muret, editors have corrected **plus** (more) to **mains** (less) (Payen is an exception).

3639 This may mean something like "living from hand to mouth" or "eating pickings."

3640 Perhaps Tristran is concealing his face (and make-up) for fear of being recognized; see 3585. In 3953, approaching the crowd on the shore, he will again keep his head down.

3663–5 Three puzzling lines. Poirion alone lets ms. 3664 stand. This activity must take place on the far side of the marsh. The correction of

hast (singular) to **hastent** (plural) is usual. Many other emendations have been proposed. See Reid ("The *Tristran* of Beroul: One Author or Two?," 284, and *Commentary*) for the grammatical and cultural reasons for the adjustments he persuasively makes to the passage (Ewert calls them "bold"), and which I adopt, e.g., **pensent** (they think) emended to **passent** (they pass). I add in support of **passent** that it is unlike both Béroul and Béroul II to concern themselves with what servants and squires may be thinking. See also the note of Braet/Raynaud de Lage II, whose reading is more traditional.

3663f The narrative of the Mal Pas scene is particularly murky. The varlets and squires pass before Tristran, somehow get across the marsh, and set up camp, seemingly without difficulty. Then come the knights (Marc's), whose horses sink into the mire and whose clothes become muddied. Afterwards Arthur arrives with his barons of the Round Table, all of whom joust before the ford, as does Arthur himself a little later (3778). Tristran calls to King Arthur and solicits his gaiters (3702–32). Then Marc arrives (3742–3). Tristran obtains his hood and gives him a fictitious history of his illness. The two kings meet and converse, wondering how the queen will deal with the Mal Pas; they agree to stay where they are and observe (3785–7). The three felons come to the ford and are misdirected by the "leper"; they are all three in the mire when Iseut arrives, escorted by Andret. Soon he and Dinas (who knows or guesses Iseut's plan) cross by a ford somewhat downstream (3876–9), and get across fairly clean. By this time Iseut is alone, except for the "leper," and is being watched by the crowd on the other side of the ford, an assemblage that includes the two kings and their barons (3880–1). Iseut prepares her palfrey, drives it across, and orders the "leper" to carry her to the far side by the walkway of planks – in full view of all the observers now gathered there.

The passage is rendered confusing and indeed incoherent by the movements of the two kings and their suites, by the fact that some groups manage to get from one side of the marsh to the other without coming to grief, and by the shifting focus on those in the mire (from the general crowd to the three felons and back again).

3684 "Drew out": from under his clothing?

3703 Here **passeor** has a different meaning from that in 3698; see Ewert II and Reid.

3712 Sc., on the near side of the ford.

3721–2 Foulet ("Marie de France," 264) suggested that this reference might put this part of the poem in the last decade of the twelfth century; it cannot, though, be very specific.

3734–5 Lines badly copied and perhaps muddled. One might conjecture "He puts them on quickly / he has sat down again on the mound." This is the understanding of Payen, Walter, Lacy, and Gregory. Braet/Raynaud de Lage translate: "les emporte" ("carries them away"). Yet there is no indication that the "leper" has left his mound to speak to Arthur, but only called him over (3714); hence his quickly returning to it is dubious. (We may imagine him coming down a few steps to take the gaiters from Arthur's squires and putting them on before sitting down again.)

3740–1 This seems to be a reprise of 3615–16 and 3625. Perhaps here, as elsewhere, such a repetition marks a break in the narrative and/or pause in the recitation.

3755–6 Why Tristran should conceal Marc's hood has not been explained. (Braet/Raynaud de Lage II take it that he also does not put on Arthur's gaiters, although he has complained of cold; but see note on 3734.) Perhaps his showing or wearing the hood might discourage others from making gifts.

3759 Lepers were excluded from society; see 1209.

3760 See the extensive notes of Braet/Raynaud de Lage II, Sandqvist, and Gregory, "Further Notes," 143–4. I adopt Gregory's emendation (see "Further Notes," 142–3).

3776 NB: *pace* Machta, 325, Tristran does *not* call his lover "la bele Yseut."

3803–6 Since the felons are in no position to give alms, this plea is ironical.

3805 Braet/Raynaud de Lage II take this as a reference to the pope.

3828 Implied is Iseut's dismounting with the help of Dinas and Andret.

3829–30 How the two royal parties get safely to the far side is not explained.

3840, 3843 This stick (**baston**), which falls into the mire, cannot be the crutch (**puiot**) still to be used by Tristran in 3928 and 3935, unless we are to imagine two words being used of the same prop, attached to Tristran's neck by a cord (3617–19). The stick/crutch may here be treacherously offered as a help to the floundering Denoalen, released when seized by the latter, then retrieved by Tristran (who draws it back by the cord).

3849 Ms.: **lemal dag**[re]**s**. This mysterious allusion has been enlisted in attempts to date the poem, a malady associated with the Siege of Acre (1190–1) sometimes being proposed. See Blakeslee, 152–7, Blakeslee and Burgess, and the note in Braet/Raynaud de Lage II. If it is indeed a reference to a "mal d'Acre," it is unique (Braet/Raynaud de Lage II). See Gregory's long note.

3866 That is, the near side, where Tristran and the queen remain.

3877 We must imagine Iseut's escorts as having by now remounted.

3885–98 Braet/Raynaud de Lage II raise, inconclusively, the question of what the spectators make of these preparations; there is no explanation offered in the text. Béroul has drawn a picture of many horses, *burdened by armed men*, coming to grief in the marshy ford; Iseut's palfrey, though, carries only its saddle and bridle, and crosses without difficulty. As for its rider, there remains the wooden walkway; but if Iseut uses it there is still a good chance of spoiling her splendid clothes (now described), and she will not take the risk. (She remounts in 3982–3.)

3899–3900 Muret's interpretation, approved by Reid and printed by most editors. See 3883–4. By now every eye is on Iseut.

3913–27 All of this dialogue can be taken as having erotic overtones, as Reid, Braet/Raynaud de Lage II, Poirion, and Burch ("Leprosy and Law") have remarked. Note **parler**, 3927.

3924–5 The "leper" not in fact having the disease, Iseut cannot catch it; her words are meant for the audience.

3931 Ladies normally rode aside; but it is essential to Iseut's plan that this time she "ride" astride. The explanatory note of Braet/Raynaud de Lage II is rather fanciful: why would even "un chevalier encore peu expérimenté" ("a still inexperienced knight") mount a horse by climbing over its rump?

3932 Presumably he smiles because he guesses Iseut's stratagem.

3935 Béroul's depiction of the arrangement is less than specific. One may imagine the "leper" passing his crutch behind himself and gripping it in both hands to support the weight of his "rider," once she is up; he is thus temporarily without the aid of his usual prop. This would account for his unsteadiness in 3936–8 and 3944–6.

3935–48 On this much-discussed passage, see Ewert.

3936 Perhaps Tristran steps forward with one foot and then drags along the other?

3947–9 Three lines with the same rhyme. Either the scribe omitted a fourth line, or he added an isolated third line (Ewert II, 7). The latter surmise seems more probable in view of 3951–2: Arthur turns that way, and the others follow suit; that the young squires would rush there first without order or leave is not likely. Reid comments that

3949 "could certainly be dispensed with." (NB: omitting it is tempting, but this would change the line-numbering and complicate subsequent references to other editions.)

3953 See note on 3640. Tristran is now approaching the edge of the marsh; the crowd there is observing him (3934–52), and despite his costume some might recognize his face. See also line 823 of the Oxford *Folie Tristran* (where Tristran reminds Isolt that once, in disguise, carrying her before spectators, "Le chef teneie mult embrune" ("I was keeping my head well down").

3957–8 Gregory takes 3958 to be direct speech; but for the "leper" to address her so, with a definite article, would be most odd. See 3868 and 3920, where he uses **dame** (= "lady") and **roïne franche** (= "queen").

3962–9 One might suspect the presence of an obscene *double entendre*, opaque to the other characters and of a piece with Tristran's fictitious genealogy of his disease, 3761f.

3971–3 Iseut was not present when Arthur and then Marc made these gifts to Tristran (3724–34, 3749–56), yet somehow knows their provenance.

3974–5 Obscure lines, much discussed. Reid's emendation of the ms. 3974, **a chat bien lit** (**lit** = "bed") to **achat berbiz**, adopted by Braet/ Raynaud de Lage and Gregory, makes sense of the pair of lines taken together: two kinds of animal, two sorts of occupation. I note that **qui past le tai** echoes the "leper's" just having served as a beast of burden: a donkey would lighten his task (see 3918).

3976 Reid proposes "and well I know it."

3982–3 That is, the squires of the kings do this. Then the two royal parties turn away from the shore of the marsh.

3986 How Tristran and Governal find one another beyond the Mal Pas is never explained.

3987–90 These must be their own mounts, those they had been riding all along since their pretended departure for Tristran's exile (2927f.), then left behind with Governal at the dwelling of Orri when Tristran went off in his leper's disguise. These lines form a supplement to the instructions in 3586–8; the detail of the Castilian origin (**de Castele**) of the horses is new, and non-essential (but supplies a rhyme).

3989 It appears that, contrary to the usual practice in jousting, Tristran and Governal carry lances with iron tips; see 4022, 4051–4. This detail seems not to have elicited critical notice.

3992–5 The movements narrated are less than clear. Tristran leaves the assembly and comes to this companion, who is awaiting him (where?)

with horses and equipment, and who turns rapidly away from there (from where?).

3999–4002 The disguise of the hero's white horse, easily recognizable, recalls 3593–6, where Tristran orders Governal to cover it. The scribe appears to have muddled the details here. Clearly **destrier** (= "war horse") is faulty, and **targe** (= "shield"), even though it rhymes, is rare, and suspect. **Coste** has been understood as **cote** = tunic (Muret, Payen, Walter, Lacy); it has not been explained how a knight was to joust while keeping a single covering at least the size of a sheet over his tunic and also his mount and shield. Nor do the editors and translators who favour **cote** deal with the improbable notion of a knight, however disguised, going into a sport as rough as the **bohort** with only a length of cloth over his tunic or, *a fortiori*, his leper's rags (see Tristran's relief when Governal earlier brought him a **hauberjon**, 1015). There is no reason why Béroul should again specify so routine a piece of equipment as a halberk.

Gregory ("Further Notes," 145–7) makes a good case for taking all four of these lines as applying to the horse and its equipment, not the rider. I adopt his emendations of 3999: **coste silie** = **costes, ilier**, **dest^rer** = **estrier**, while making all three substantives plural, and go on to observe that the covering mentioned in the following line need not be visualized as one large piece of black serge cloth draped over Bel Joëor (a most impractical arrangement). What is being sketchily described is a trapper (or caparison), in the usual two pieces covering the front and rear halves of the animal, being joined under the saddle but allowing access to the girth and, indispensably, to the stirrups. It would descend to the horse's white fetlocks (necessarily still visible, but they in themselves would not identify the animal). The two large panels would be secured by the saddle, a common arrangement in the period, and by ties at chest and rump. Another piece of black cloth, **un noir voil**, is wrapped about the animal's face, and is no doubt held in place by the straps of the bridle. Thus the white steed is entirely disguised, head and body.

As for Tristran, he would have no reason to veil his own head and hair, if he had a halberk with a mail coif or ventail, or else wore a helmet; at a distance a helmet with its usual nasal would make identifying him difficult for spectators and opponents alike. Granted that Béroul mentions helmet no more than he does halberk; he also does not state that Governal brings his own sword with him, but by 4006 each man has one (Tristran having worn his all the while under his leper's disguise, 3575–6).

Thus the most likely way of envisioning the scene, confusingly depicted by the poet, is that Governal has brought Tristran's white horse covered fore and aft with two large pieces of heavy cloth joined together, descending to the fetlocks.

4003–4 Tristran has Iseut's pennon (mentioned in 3603), which she will recognize (4033).

4009. La Blanche Lande: a name (or its equivalents in other languages) often encountered. Here it designates a manor in Cornwall, near the **Mal Pas**, attested in the mid-thirteenth century. See Padel, "The Cornish Background," 60–1.

4020 Ms. **rote** cannot be "crowd" (as most translators, as well as Reid, and Ewert in his glossary). What crowd could there be, given that this single pair of unknown knights is just coming into sight from a distance? Disguised as they are, they still have good reason not to mingle with the others on the main track. For **rote** see 1529 and 1618. Payen, accurately: they "s'écartent du chemin."

4020–44 See Braet/Raynaud de Lage II on this, Tristran's only participation in knightly combat.

4021 Ms.: **pres** (= "close to them"); emendation of Ewert and Reid, followed by Gregory. See 4037. (Payen oddly translates "l'écu brandi," his 3991 [shields were not brandished]; Braet/Raynaud de Lage give **pres** but translate "au poing"[= "in hand"]). The shield, when not in use, was slung over the back; these riders are holding theirs ready for action.

4022 For **fers** (= "iron tips"), see note on 3989. Governal's pennon is not described.

4025–6 The abrupt change of subject suggests an inversion of the lines (not heretofore noted).

4026–7 The two kings speak more of the two approaching riders, who bear their arms so well, than of their own two bands of followers (**compaignes** = companies of knights, not **compaignes** = "épouses" [= spouses] as Payen, his 3997).

4031 Ewert II calls this the first manoeuvre in a tourney, when each knight seeks an opponent.

4033–5 Iseut easily identifies them, having sent the pennon to Tristran herself (4003–4). By now she is remounted (3982–3) and, with Brengain, has moved off to the side of the lists, where she can see and be seen. When Tristran strikes Andret he throws him down at her palfrey's feet. (This must be the second Andret; see note on 2870.)

4035–59 Here Andret and also Marc's denouncing forester (see 1837f.) are seen as companions of Arthur's knights. (We note that the forester, killed by Perinis in 2759–62, has seemingly returned to life.)

4045–8 The poet implies that Governal recognizes the forester and takes revenge, yet Governal was absent when the forester came to the shelter, went off to Marc, and returned with him (1838–2054).

4052 Ms.: **cuir** (= leather). The line is puzzling. Sandqvist would emend to **cuer**, yet this seems unlikely on anatomical grounds. Reid suggests "a part of the lance below the blade." The leather hand-grip has also been proposed (Lacy, Braet/Raynaud de Lage II, Gregory). (This would implausibly imply nearly the whole length of the lance passing through the forester's body.) Payen and Walter do not deal with **cuir**. Muret/Defourques, glossary, **cuir**: "peau humaine." Braet (*Béroul, Le Roman de Tristan, version complète en français moderne*) translates "la peau." Poirion (*Tristan et Yseut, les premières versions européennes*) resigns himself to "l'acier ressort de l'autre côté avec le cuir." Perhaps the word designates leather thongs attaching the iron tip to the shaft?

4061 How Gawain recognizes Marc's forester is not explained.

4066 The king is Arthur, more prominent than Marc in this episode.

4075 Muret, glossary: "tenir la droite de qqn, chevaucher à sa droite"; Ewert, glossary, **destroier**: "ride on the right hand of." All previous translators seemingly have accepted this reading, yet it is highly dubious. Iseut would again be riding side-saddle, with both legs on the near (= left) side of her palfrey and her feet on the foot-rest. If Arthur rides on her right, she perforce has her back to him and must talk to him, if at all, over her shoulder – an uncomfortable arrangement. Far more convenient would be for Arthur to act as Iseut's squire, managing his own mount with his left hand (as he would do in combat, and as a modern riding instructor does with a neophyte's mount) and holding the queen's rein with his right (as a squire would do with a **destrier**, whence the name, and as a modern mounted groom does when leading a race-horse). This arrangement is earlier implied in 2770–2849, where Tristran holds the rein of Iseut's palfrey and converses with her at length as they ride towards Marc. He even draws her close to him and embraces her – scarcely possible if she has her back to him.

Godefroy's dictionary does not include **destroier** in the sense of "accompany" or "lead," but gives **destrer**: "v.a.: être à droite de, accompagner," yet, contradictorily, **destré** past participle, "ayant à sa droite." (His numerous citations, especially that from *Perceforest*, unmistakably have ladies riding on the right of their escorts.) The dictionary of Tobler-Lommatzsch does give the term, but ambiguously: "auf der rechten Seite begleiten." (To accompany on whose right side?) The word does not figure in the glossary of M^2 (1922); it does in M^4 (1967) as, oddly, "tenir la droite de qqn. chevaucher à sa droite." This erroneous reading of the line seems never to have been challenged previously.

4080–4113 Braet/Raynaud de Lage II draw attention to the courtly tone marking this scene: the exchange of courtesies and of gifts, the rich clothing, the musical instruments, etc.

4081 Ms. **corbel** (= crows); standard correction since Muret (but not in Ewert or Gregory). The implication may be "even the tent-ropes." No expense is spared; see 4080–4103.

4086 Ms. **vestue**: a repetition of the preceding rhyme-word, hence suspect. The emendation to **sa drue** goes back to Muret. Braet/Raynaud de Lage print the apparently contradictory 4123–4 (knights have brought their wives) – but perhaps the conjectural **drue** can be taken as a general term for "beloved."

4087–9 That is, anyone who did not join in the nocturnal hunt still heard the horn-calls; these may announce the pursuit (see Ewert, Glossary) or the stag being at bay (Ewert, Commentary), or perhaps the return from a successful hunt (Reid). (The interpretations of Walter and Gregory, taking **ot** as the third person preterite of **avoir** (to have), are wide of the mark.)

4089 The two royal parties have settled down near each other.

4111–16 This passage is particularly rich in sound-effects.

4114–15 Reid's interpretation ("On the Text," 265), which I follow, is generally accepted (but not by Walter or Braet/Raynaud de Lage II).

4115–20 If the pre-dawn thunder betokens coming heat, and the sun is already warm by Prime (the first hour of the day; see note on 873), then 4120 is puzzling: can **frime** here have its usual sense of "hoar-frost" (Ewert, Glossary)? Lacy gives "dew," which is far less unlikely.

4123–4 Since the kingdom is Cornwall, the **cort** must be Marc's court, i.e., wherever he is.

4126 Here the king is Arthur, who will preside.

4127–8 Inverting these lines, as I have done, gives a more logical order: first the length of silk is viewed from a distance, spread out on the grass, then from closer up so that the small embroidered motifs can be seen.

4134 mases remains problematical. One might conjecture the tips of ceremonial maces, with relics enclosed.

4135 Ms.: **S or lepailes les orent mises** No subject is expressed; a "they" is implied. See Ewert and Braet/Raynaud de Lage II. Given the negative quality of the whole phrase, **les** is best emended to **nes** I take the line as meaning: "There were no relics in all of Cornwall that had not been placed on the brocade."

4141–69 Arthur, opening the proceedings, reveals at once that he considers Iseut to be the innocent victim of slander, apparently unaware that Marc and the felons had themselves seen Tristran's blood on the floor and in the bed of the royal chamber (767–80). His speech effectively prohibits any reference to the bedroom scene, even by those who had been eyewitnesses of the evidence. (In fact, they play no part in the whole oath-taking episode, although they will be named and admonished by Gawain, 4238–9.)

Arthur's tone to his fellow sovereign is highly peremptory.

4158 Ms.: **oiez** (imperative; "hear"); Gregory argues tellingly for the future **orez**. As for **qui ara tort**, both Ewert and Reid find it obscure, as do I. Perhaps we should understand: "who will be [proven] wrong" (sc. Iseut or her accusers)?

4163–6 This is the wording of the oath Iseut is to swear; it turns on her relations with Marc's nephew alone.

4179–81 See the note in Braet/Raynaud de Lage II on the feebleness on Marc's quasi-apology.

4185 Reid interprets "close to them," Gregory "close between the two of them." Other scholars (Lacy, Braet/Raynaud de Lage II, Walter, Payen) understand that each of the kings holds Iseut by one of her hands. I find this reading persuasive, and suggest that it may have textual support (or at least may be anticipated thematically) in Iseut's bad dream after Marc discovered the lovers in their bower and spared them. She dreamt of two hungry lions; see note to 2072: "Each was holding her by the hand."

4189–90 Arthur's physical closeness to Iseut is expressive of his more sympathetic attitude.

4191–6 Arthur, taking charge, summons Iseut to swear to the seemliness of Tristran's love for both his uncle and his uncle's spouse. His language is courtly and general; Iseut's oath (4205–16) is crude and specific.

4197–4216 Iseut's oath turns from the nature of Tristran's love to her own experience of the preceding day. It also deftly avoids answering Arthur's charge, while being in appearance more inclusive.

4201 On St Hilaire and laxity in the matter of oaths, see Jonin, *Personnages*, 344–8. The poet may have chosen the name for the rhyme; but this particular saint counselled specifically in favour of simplicity in oath-taking and against equivocation. Braet/Raynaud de Lage II are sceptical on this point.

4217–31 Public opinion, voiced in this unison chorus, entirely favours Iseut; the spectators will repeat almost verbatim (4225–30) her statement in 4205–8, and call her accusers **fel** (4222).

4219 Ms.: **sifiere eniure**; **eniure** has been variously understood. It is not evident why **fiere** should be read as an adjective describing Iseut (its usual meaning is "proud" or "arrogant"). Ewert proposes that it may have adverbial force. It is not even clear whether **jure** is noun or verb. Reid ("On the Text," 266–7) proposes **enjure = injure** and interprets: "so cruel a wrong! So well has she afterwards justified herself against it!" This interpretation, although bold, does make sense both in itself and as an introduction to the following lines. I add that such a reading leads seamlessly into the crowd's unanimous siding with Iseut against her accusers, now designated as **li fel** (for **felon**, 4221).

The "wrong" or "injustice" may be the original charge, or else her now having to refute it in public.

4225 Another problematical line, for the oath-taking involves two kings (Arthur and Marc) and two nephews (Gawain and Tristran, although the latter is not named in Iseut's oath). Certainly a specific exception for the king (Marc) *and* his nephew is not acceptable; the reference must be to Arthur and Gawain (Reid). The **fors du/de** (= "except for") are also questionable. One should note that in the preceding passage, 4184–4206, **fors** without **de** appears thrice in initial position, and clearly bearing the meaning "except for." Gregory understands the unusual **fors de/du** in 4225 as "in addition to," as in the *Anglo-Norman Dictionary*, I think rightly. The **de/du** in 4225 may well indicate a different function of the preposition.

See also the substantial commentaries of Ewert, Reid, Braet/Raynaud de Lage II, and Gregory.

This line figures in the unanimous response (4219–31) of the two combined audiences, repeating the substance of what they have just heard Iseut swear before them all, including the listening king and his nephew.

4229 Terce: the second canonical hour: mid-morning. The word **guez** is oddly plural ("fords").

4232 Ms.: **l imes** or **l inies** or **l unes art**[us] has been transcribed in several ways. **Li rois Artus** (as Ewert, Walter, Lacy, Braet/Raynaud de Lage) is to be rejected, and for a reason that has not heretofore been noted: Arthur does not now rise to his feet, since like Marc he has been standing beside Iseut and holding her hand before and during her oath-taking (4183–5). All other witnesses have been seated (4183–4). We can take Gawain, now rising here, to be Arthur's spokesman; it is he who will if necessary come spurring to the queen's defence from wherever he may be (4241–6), and he whom she thanks in 4247. (She thanks Arthur separately in 4251.)

4237–40 Gawain now pronounces the names of the three felons, and threatens them.

4241–6 This promise, with vocabulary, verb tenses, rhyme t^{er}**re** and g^{er}**re**, and all, is very close to Tristran's in 2689–91 (cited by Reid). The similarity justifies the correction of ms.

4242 Q^{ui} **l** mai^n**tenist** (= "Which he would maintain") to **Que m'en tenist** (= "That would prevent me") made by Muret, M^4, Walter, Lacy, and Braet/Raynaud de Lage. In 4245, all editors have hitherto retained the present indicative first person plural **allons** (= "we go") of the ms., as do Braet/Raynaud de Lage, Gregory, and Walter (but see Reid's persuasive note). The sense is: "Wherever I am and whatever I may be doing, nothing would prevent me from acting on an appeal from the queen."

4256 Arthur, too, brands the accusing barons as **felon** in Marc's hearing.

4266 Tristran is in the vicinity somewhere, having disappeared after 4068–9; his enemies will soon learn that he and Governal are nearby, presumably staying with Dinas (4301).

4285–6 Like Ewert, Walter, and Braet/Raynaud de Lage, I invert the ms. lines to give a more natural succession of ideas: "Tristran hides, I know where; Tristran is very foxy; when the king goes off … " Malpertuis: the fox's den in the *Roman de Renart* (named in Branch Va, the oldest branch, dated around 1174–7; see Braet/Raynaud de Lage II, note on 4285). The word after Tristran is clearly **set**: "knows about." Gregory gives **fet** ("does"), but **fet de** plus place-name is unusual.

4287 The expression **congié prendre** certainly does not mean "to say farewell" (as Braet/Raynaud de Lage, Walter, and Lacy). The subject of the verb must be Tristran; why would he go into the royal chamber – and in Marc's absence – merely to take leave? Gregory offers "for his amorous assignation." **Congié prendre** is a euphemism similar to **parler** when used of an assignation; see 4283, 4330, and note on 657. For possible emendations to **congié** see Muret and Reid (but taking the ms. ^{con}**gie** as standing for **son gre** and hence as a scribal error for **son sez/ses sez** ["take his pleasure"] is paleographically dubious).

4292–3 An anticipation of 4422–3.

4314 Every emendation proposed is open to challenge. Like Lacy and Gregory, I accept Sandqvist's as the most economical solution.

It seems that the **pertus** is an aperture in the chamber wall, roughly at garden level (since no steps are mentioned), narrow (so as to make entry impossible) but still wide enough that anyone moving past it could be noticed from within (4322). The opening, if uncovered, permits a view into the interior. The stationary head of Godoïne will cast a visible shadow on the curtain, which he will of course not have moved aside completely (4428, 4461–2).

4316 The definite article of **la cortine** implies that this is the normal arrangement.

4319–26 The spy's plan, not exposed sequentially, is that one of the three felons will cut and sharpen a stick, take it along with him, enter the garden early and quietly, get close to the window-slit, and catch the curtain with the thorny twig. The curtain is of course on the inner side of the opening (4316), and the wall (being of stone) necessarily fairly thick; hence the instruction concerning the length of the twig the observer is to take with him (4323).

4322 Ms.: **fors la fenestre**; Reid proposes emending to **fors a senestre**: "let no one go except to the left." So also in Gregory ("making sure you keep to the left").

4322–9 I understand: "Approach from the left, stop just before reaching the opening, prick the curtain with the branch and push it aside, cautiously, so that you can clearly see into the chamber." Usually **sachier** means "to pull," but it is difficult to grasp how *pulling* the curtain aside towards the observer (as Gregory) could be performed inconspicuously.

For **sache** (4327), Ewert in II proposes translating by a neutral verb: "move the curtain gently over the opening … "; Walter and Braet/Raynaud de Lage modernize by the equally general *écarte* ("move away").

4323–4 These lines are out of sequence; necessarily the spy is to bring the tool with him.

4328 Ms.: **c'on ne l'estache**. Reid conjectures **c'on ne le sache**, "in such a way that they do not know it, without anyone's knowing." Gregory accepts this, as do I. Other editors understand that the curtain is not/ never fastened; but how could the spy be sure of this?

4347 Béroul II seemingly forgets that we know who Perinis is.

4350 That Béroul II had in mind St Lubin, venerated in the diocese of Chartres, is most improbable, unless here the poet or scribe was quite indifferent to geography. A royal progress from Cornwall across the Channel to the Chartres region, decided for the next day, could scarcely be organized at a moment's notice. I conjecture a local (and quite possibly garbled) place-name.

4352 The night cannot be "pitch-dark" (Gregory) or "noire" (Payen, Walter, Braet/Raynaud de Lage) or even "very dark" (Lacy). "Moonless" might come close, since there is still sufficient light for people to walk, ride, and hunt with dogs. Tristran is able to recognize both Godoïne (4356–7, 4396–7) and, at a distance, Denoalen (4369–71). It is summer; the iris is growing thickly (4318); the recent **escondit** took place in hot weather (4115, 4119). In the latitude of southern Britain (and of Normandy, for that matter), the summer nights are short, and dusky rather than black. (Both Béroul and Béroul II may very well have travelled in Cornwall.)

4353–68 Tristran, hiding in the thicket, and on foot, naturally moves more slowly than Godoïne, who is presumably mounted like Denoalen (4371f.).

4373 This is the posture of a hunter at stand, steadying himself against a support (see 1694–5). Walter and Lacy take it that Tristran hides behind the apple tree; Payen and Gregory ("Further Notes," 148) understand that Tristran has climbed up into the tree. The first of these conjectures is not impossible, the second most unlikely: climbing a tree, while encumbered with a sword at the least, would be awkward, and would probably attract the attention of the approaching rider (the latter being close enough to be recognizable) and his greyhounds. And if Tristran were to jump down from the tree it would certainly make the approaching horse shy. Tristran, in ambush, has every interest in being still until the last moment.

4381 The **desfublez** of the ms. should be retained, as most editors do; Tristran removes his hooded cloak prior to going into action (see 1250, 1254, 1983). We note that he puts it on again in 4406–7, and doffs it in Iseut's chamber, 4425. (Gregory proposes emending to **desfustez**, "leapt down from the tree," assuming that Tristran had gone up into it; see my note on 4373.)

4414f The recurrence of **voir** ("to see") is striking, and foreshadows the spy Godoïne's being shot in the eye.

4417 Ms.: **vint** ("came"). Given **vit** ("saw") twice in 4414–15, and **voit** ("sees") once in 4416, I take the word here (with Gregory alone) to be an error for **vit**. The topic of this whole passage is what the spy observes. He has a clear view of all that is in the chamber: no *man* except Perinis, but he does notice Brengain there. (And why would

Brengain *come* into the chamber of her mistress, comb still in hand, after having combed her hair – elsewhere? It is noteworthy that the queen does not enter the room but is already there, 4426–7.) The only person the spy sees entering is Tristran (4421).

4420f Tristran enters with his trophy, his two arrows, and his unstrung bow. He must take Iseut's meaning from her unexpected words and manner. He follows her instruction to bend his bow and give a demonstration of how he goes about bracing it; he is also to make sure that the bow-string is not tangled, and nock an arrow. Understanding that something is troubling her, he glances up, detects an observer at the window, draws his braced bow, turns towards the wall, and shoots.

For an analysis of this final episode of the fragment, see Sargent-Baur, "Accidental Symmetry." My remarks on p. 342 should be modified; I there overstated certain similarities between Marc-as-spy in the first preserved scene and Godoïne-as-spy in the episode before the manuscript breaks off. Marc certainly watched and overheard the lovers from above, in a tree; as for Godoïne's own observation post, it might be somewhat elevated (e.g., on an earthen bank), but nothing like tree height is implied (*pace* Maddox, 187).

It is noteworthy that Iseut catches sight of the spy's shadow as she rises to greet Tristran; Béroul does not account for this person's being within her field of vision and so distracting her from greeting her lover normally. Only in 4459–61 does Tristran realize that her odd behaviour is the result of something she has seen; he looks up and sees it also.

I add here that "looks up" presumably means that he raises his eyes from the bow and arrow in his hands. (He must turn to shoot, 4472.)

4422–4 What Tristran brings with him corresponds to 4492–3, with the addition of Denoalen's tresses.

4440 The first person plural, here and in 4456, is a reminder of Brengain's presence.

4443 "He takes his decision" or perhaps "He takes her meaning."

4447–9 The consensus of commentators and translators is that if Godoïne gets away alive he will cause a deadly war to *resume* between Marc and Iseut. But there has been no war *between* them, only strife fomented by others, specifically the three felons, on their account.

4457 This line closely echoes 4441; in both, Tristran proceeds by stops and starts as he struggles to grasp Iseut's ambiguous orders.

4462 Tristran cannot identify the watcher hidden behind the curtain (no more can Iseut); but he guesses that it is one of the three felons (4466–7); he well knows that by now only two remain.

4463–71 Braet/Raynaud de Lage draw attention to the glaring inappropriateness of this prayer, combining as it does Tristran's wish for an accurate bow-shot directed at one of his Cornish enemies with an evocation of God's (i.e., Christ's) sacrifice of himself for mankind.
4472–7 This feat of archery has given rise to divers interpretations, several stemming from readings of the word at the head of 4473, **S oueut/S onent**. (For a listing of some of these, see Sargent-Baur, "Accidental Symmetry," 344–5, appendix A. I there postulate that the word in question cannot bear the meanings "repeatedly" or "slowly" or "vigorously" sometimes assigned to it.) This must be one more scribal blunder, a meaningless substitution for **Son arc** ("his bow"); see Reid and Gregory.

Béroul has informed us of Tristran's prowess as an archer (1279–80); as soon as the hero and Governal have rescued Iseut from the lepers and fled into the forest, he undertakes to feed the three of them with game, using a bow and arrows supplied by his **mestre**. This is seemingly the equipment that he will use henceforth, to be supplemented for a time by the **arc qui ne faut** (1752). (The latter is a hidden trap set to fire when disturbed, not a normal hunting weapon and certainly not one that Tristran carries with him in this scene, as Maddox, 188.)
4484 This is the last sequential line of the text; **Bleciez** … at the bottom of the folio is the catchword for the missing next page.

Bibliography

Béroul's celebrated romance has generated quantities of editions, translations, and studies, in several languages and with more appearing each year; see "Béroul" in the annual *Bibliographical Bulletin of the International Arthurian Society* (Middleton, WI: A–R Editions). The titles listed below designate a number of works that have been useful in the preparation of the present English translation and commentary thereon. A more substantial bibliography than the one offered here is to be found at the end of the Critical Edition; the works listed below are limited to those accessible to readers of English and Modern French. A more comprehensive bibliography to 1980, and including works by other authors, was drawn up by David J. Shirt: *The Old French Tristran Poems: A Bibliographical Guide*, in the series Research Bibliographies and Checklists (London: Grant and Cutler, 1980). As its title announces, the focus therein is by no means limited to Béroul. Less wide-ranging, and more recent, is the bibliography appearing at the end of vol. II of *Béroul: Tristran et Iseut, Poème du XIIe siècle*, edited with a facing Modern French version and copious notes by Herman Braet and Guy Raynaud de Lage (1999).

1. Editions and Translations

Braet, Herman. *Béroul, Le Roman de Tristan, version complète en français moderne.* Gand: Edition Scientifiques, E. Story-Scientia SPRL, 1974.

Braet, Herman, and Guy Raynaud de Lage. *Béroul, Tristran et Iseut.* 2 v. Paris and Louvain: Peeters, 1989. (I: Edition and Translation; II: Notes and Commentaries. 2nd edition revised, 1999.) Old French with facing Modern French translation.

Ewert, A[lfred]. *The Romance of Tristran by Béroul.* 2 v. Oxford: Blackwell, 1939, 1970.

Gregory, Stewart. *The Romance of Tristran by Béroul*. Amsterdam and Atlanta: Rodopi, 1992. Old French with facing English translation.

Jonin, Pierre. *Béroul, le Roman de Tristan, traduit de l'ancien français*. CFMA Traductions 20. Paris: Champion, 1974. Modern French.

Lacroix, Daniel, and Philippe Walter. *Tristan et Iseut, les poèmes français, la saga norroise*. Paris: Librairie Générale Française, 1989. Béroul's text with facing Modern French translation by Walter; the *Saga* appears in Modern French translation by Lacroix.

Lacy, Norris J. *Béroul's Tristran*. In *Early French Tristan Poems* I, ed. Norris J. Lacy. Cambridge: D.S. Brewer, 1998. Facing English translation of Béroul and also of the two *Folies Tristan* of Oxford and Berne, with English translation. (Vol. II includes the *Tristan* of Thomas, the lay of *Chevrefeuille* of Marie de France, and the episodic poems *Tristan Rossignol* and *Tristan Menestrel*, all provided with English versions.)

Mermier, Guy R. *Béroul: Tristan and Yseut*. New York, Berne, Frankfurt, and Paris: Peter Lang, 1987. English translation alone.

Muret, Ernest. (M0; "Muret"). *Le Roman de Tristan par Béroul et un anonyme, poème du XIIe siècle*. Paris: Société des Anciens Textes Français, 1903.

– (M1). *Béroul, le Roman de Tristan, poème du XIIe siècle*. CFMA 12. Paris: Champion, 1913. 2nd edition revised, 1922.

– (M2). *Béroul, le Roman de Tristan, poème du XIIe siècle*. CFMA 12. Paris: Champion, 1922.

– (M3). 3rd edition revised, 1928. CFMA 12.

– (M4). 4th edition revised by L.M. Defourques, 1947. CFMA 12.

Payen, Jean-Charles. *Le Tristan de Béroul*. In *Les Tristan en vers*, ed. Jean-Charles Payen. Paris: Garnier, 1974. Modern French above, Old French below.

Poirion, Daniel. *Béroul, Tristan et Yseut*. Paris: Imprimerie Nationale, 1989. Revised and reprinted in *Tristan et Yseut, les premières versions européennes*, ed. Christiane Marchello-Nizia. Bibliothèque de la Pléiade. Paris: Gallimard, 1995. This last encompasses the romances of Béroul and Thomas, the *Chèvrefeuille* of Marie de France, the Oxford and Berne *Folies* (all these presented with Modern French above and Old French below). As well, the volume includes Modern French translations of versions written in other European languages: those in Middle High German of Eilhart von Oberge and of Gottfried von Strassburg, the *First Continuation* of Ulrich von Türheim, and the *Second Continuation* of Heinrich von Freiberg. Here too in Modern French are the saga of *Tristram og Isönd* by Brother Robert (a translation into Old Norse prose of Thomas's poem) and the Middle English *Sir Tristrem*; parts of the story in the Italian *Tavola ritonda* and in other tongues – including Czech – appear in French translation.

Varvaro, Alberto. *Il "roman de Tristran" di Béroul.* Turin: Bottega d'Erasmo, 1963.
– *Béroul's Romance of Tristan.* Trans. John C. Barnes. Manchester: Manchester University Press, 1972.
Walter, Philippe. *See* Lacroix, above.

2. Studies Cited in the Notes to the Present Translation

Batany, Jean. "Le manuscrit de Béroul: Un texte difficile et un univers mental qui nous dérange." In *La Légende de Tristan au Moyen Age,* ed. D. Buschinger. Göppingen: Kümmerle, 1982, 35–48.
Baumgartner, Emmanuèle. "Jeux et rimes et roman arthurien." *Romania* 103 (1982): 550–60.
Blakeslee, Merritt R. "*Mal d'Acre, Malpertuis* and the Date of Beroul's *Tristran.*" *Romania* 106 (1985): 145–72.
Blakeslee, Merritt R., and Glyn S. Burgess. "*Dagres, d'Acre, degiez*: Note sur le vers 3849 du Tristran de Béroul." *Romania* 107 (1986): 536–40.
Bromiley, G[eoffrey] N. "A Note on Béroul's Foresters." *Tristania* 1 (1975): 39–46.
– "Andret and the Tournament Episode in Béroul's *Tristran.*" *Medium Ævum* 46 (1977): 181–95.
– *See* Hunt, Tony, and Geoffrey Bromiley.
Burch, Sally L. "'Tu consenz lor cruauté': The Canonical Background to the Barons' Accusation in Béroul's *Roman de Tristan.*" *Tristania* 20 (2001): 17–30.
– "Leprosy and Law in Béroul's *Roman de Tristan.*" *Viator* 38 (2007): 141–54.
Ditmas, E.M.R. "The Invention of Tintagel." *BBSIA* 23 (1971): 131–6.
– "Béroul the Minstrel." *Reading Medieval Studies* 8 (1982): 34–74.
Ewert, A[lfred]. "On the Text of Béroul's *Tristran.*" In *Studies in French Language and Mediaeval Literature Presented to Professor Mildred K. Pope by Pupils, Colleagues and Friends.* Manchester: Manchester University Press, 1939, 89–98.
Foulet, Lucien. "Marie de France et la légende de Tristran." *Zeitschrift für romanische Philologie* 32 (1908): 257–89.
– "Sire, Messire (I)." *Romania* 71 (1950): 1–48.
Gregory, Stewart. "Notes on the Text of Beroul's *Tristan.*" *French Studies* 35 (1981): 1–18.
– "Further Notes on the Text of Béroul's *Tristan* (Pt. One)." *French Studies* 42 (1988): 1–20 and 129–49.
Henry, A. "Du subjonctif d'imminence contrecarrée à un passage du *Tristan* de Bèroul." *Romania* 73 (1952): 392–407.

– "Sur les vers 320–338 du 'Tristan' de Bérould." In *Mélanges d'études romanes du moyen âge et de la Renaissance offerts à M. Jean Rychner.* Travaux de Linguistique et de Littérature 16 1. Strasbourg, 1978, 209–15.

– "Pour le commentaire du 'Tristan' de Béroul." In *Studies in Medieval French Language and Literature Presented to Brian Woledge in Honour of His 80th Birthday,* ed. S. Burch North. Publications Romanes et Françaises 180. Geneva: Droz, 1987, 59–65.

Holden, Anthony. "Note sur la langue de Béroul." *Romania* 89 (1968): 388–99.

Hunt, Tony. "Textual Notes on Béroul and Thomas: Some Problems of Interpretation and Emendation." *Tristania* 1 (1975): 19–38.

Hunt, Tony, and Geoffrey Bromiley. "The Tristan Legend in Old French Verse." In *Arthurian Literature in the Middle Ages IV: The Arthur of the French,* ed. Glyn S. Burgess and Karen Pratt. Cardiff: University of Wales Press, 2006, 112–18.

Illingworth, Richard N. "The Episode of the Ambiguous Oath in Beroul's *Tristran.*" *Zeitschrift für romanische Philologie* 106 (1990): 22–42.

– "The Composition of the *Tristran* of Béroul." *Arthurian Literature* 18 (2001): 1–75.

Jonin, Pierre. *Les personnages féminins dans les romans français de Tristan au XIIe siècle: Etude des influences contemporaines.* Publications des Annales de La Faculté des Lettres, Aix-en-Provence, 22. Gap: Ophrys, 1958.

Lecoy, Félix. "Sur les vers 1461–1462 du *Tristan* de Béroul." *Romania* 80 (1959): 82–5.

– Review of Reid, *The Tristran of Béroul,* in *Romania* 93 (1972): 575–6.

Le Gentil, Pierre. "L'épisode du Morois et la signification du Tristan de Béroul." In *Studia philologica et litteraria in honore L. Spitzer.* Berne: Francke, 1958, 267–74.

Legge, Mary Dominica. "The Unerring Bow." *Medium Aevum* 25 (1956): 79–83.

– "Place-Names and the Date of Beroul." *Medium Ævum* 28 (1969): 171–4.

Loth, Joseph. "Le Cornwall et le roman de Tristan." *Contributions à l'étude des romans de la Table Ronde.* Paris: Champion, 1912; *Revue Celtique* 34 (1913): 365–96; and *Revue Celtique* 37 (1917–19): 317ff.

Machta, Insaf. *Poétique de la ruse dans les récits tristaniens français du XIIe siècle.* Paris: Champion, 2010.

Maddox, Donald. "L'auto-réécriture béroulienne et ses fonctions." In *Le Roman de Tristan: Le maschere di Béroul,* ed. Rosanna Brusegan. Rome: Salerno, 2001, 181–90.

Ménard, Philippe. "L'art de Béroul." In *Le Roman de Tristan: Le maschere di Béroul,* ed. Rosanna Brusegan. Rome: Salerno, 2001, 221–39.

Moignet, Gérard. "Remarques sur le pronon personnel régime dans la syntaxe du 'Tristan' de Béroul." In *Mélanges de langue et de littérature médiévale offerts à Pierre Le Gentil*. Paris: SEDES and EDU, 1973, 561–8.

Newstead, Helaine. "King Mark of Cornwall." *Romance Philology* 11 (1957–8): 155–66.

Padel. Oliver J. "The Cornish Background to the Tristan Stories." *Cambridge Medieval Celtic Studies* 1 (1981): 53–81.

– "Beroul's Geography and Patronage." *Reading Medieval Studies* 9 (1983): 84–94.

Raynaud de Lage, Guy. "Faut-il attribuer à Béroul tout le Tristan?" *Moyen Age* 64 (1958): 249–70. Rpt. in Raynaud de Lage, *Les premiers romans français et autres études littéraires et linguistiques*. Publications Romanes et Françaises 128. Geneva: Droz, 1976, 103–19.

– "Faut-il attribuer à Béroul tout le Tristan? (suite et fin)." *Moyen Age* 70 (1964): 33–8. Rpt. in Raynaud de Lage, *Les premiers romans français*, 121–5.

Reid, T[homas] B[ertram] W[allace]. "On the Text of the *Tristran* of Beroul." In *Medieval Miscellany Presented to Eugène Vinaver*. Manchester and New York: Manchester University Press, 1965, 263–88.

– "The *Tristran* of Beroul: One Author or Two?" *Modern Language Review* 60 (1965): 352–8.

– *The "Tristran" of Béroul: A Textual Commentary*. Oxford: Blackwell, 1972.

Sandqvist, Sven. *Notes textuelles sur le Roman de Tristan de Béroul*. Etudes romanes de Lund 39. Lund: CWK Gleerup, 1984.

Sargent-Baur, Barbara N. "Between Fabliau and Romance: Love and Rivalry in Béroul's *Tristran*." *Romania* 105 (1984): 292–311.

– "Truth, Half-Truth, Untruth: Béroul's Telling of the Tristran Story." In *The Craft of Fiction*, ed. L. Arrathoon. Rochester, MI: Solaris Press, 1984, 393–421.

– "Béroul's *Tristran* and the Praise of *Folie*." *Bibliographical Bulletin of the International Arthurian Society* 38 (1986): 289–97.

– "La dimension morale dans le *Roman de Tristan* de Béroul." *Cahiers de Civilisation Médiévale* 31 (1988): 49–56.

– "Accidental Symmetry: The First and Last Episodes of Béroul's *Roman de Tristan*." *Neophilologus* 88 (2004): 335–51.

Skårup, Povl. *Les premières zones de la proposition en ancien français. Essai de syntaxe de position*. *Revue romane*. Special issue 6. Copenhagen, 1975.

Vinaver, Eugène. "Pour le commentaire du vers 1650 du *Tristan* de Béroul." In *Studies in Medieval French Presented to Alfred Ewert*. Oxford: Blackwell, 1961, 90–5.

– "Remarques sur quelques vers de Béroul." In *Studies in Medieval Literature and Languages in Memory of Frederick Whitehead*. Manchester: Manchester University Press, 1973, 341–52.

3. Other Texts and Reference Works Cited

Brody, Saul N. *The Disease of the Soul: Leprosy in Medieval Literature*. Ithaca and London: Cornell University Press, 1974.

Godefroy, Frédéric. *Dictionnaire de l'ancienne langue française*. Paris: Vieweg, 1881–1902.

Greimas, Algirdas Julien. *Dictionnaire de l'ancien français*. Paris: Larousse-Bordas, 2001.

Milin, Gaël. *Le roi Marc aux oreilles de cheval*. PRF 197. Geneva: Droz, 1991.

Morawski, Joseph. *Proverbes français antérieurs au XVe siècle*. Paris: Champion, 1925.

Stone, L., W. Rothwell, et al. *Anglo-Norman Dictionary*. London: Maney (Modern Humanities Research Association), 1977–92; 2nd edition (A–E, ed. W. Rothwell), 2005–.

Tobler, A., and E. Lommatzsch. *Altfranzösisches Wörterbuch*. Berlin: Steiner, 1925–.

Index of Proper Names

The names are reproduced as they appear in the Critical Edition.

Agres 3849 (*mal dagres*). Sometimes taken as an allusion to the crusaders' siege of Acre, Syria, in 1190–1

Adan 1134. Adam

André, Saint 3132. Patron saint of Scotland, whose relics were venerated at St Andrews

Andret, Andrez. Seemingly the name of two characters, one a baron at Marc's court, 2870, 3783, 3877, the other an opponent of Tristran at the Mal Pas, 4035, 4039, 4041

Artur, Artus 649, 684, etc. King Arthur

Baudas 3904. Baghdad

Bel Joëor (le) 3997. Tristran's steed

Berous 1268, 1790. Béroul

Blanche Lande (la), la Lande Blanche 2653, 3268, 3298, 4009, 4085. A heath in Cornwall

Brengain 340, 347, etc. Iseut's maid and companion

Bretaigne 2247. Brittany

Caharés 3076. Carhaix in Brittany. *See* Tresmor

Carduel 650, 684. Carlisle in Cumberland, North of England

Carloon 3758. Caerleon (upon Usk? in Wales)

Castele 3987. Castile, in Spain

Chatons 1939. Cato the Elder, to whom moralizing aphorisms were attributed in the Middle Ages

Cinglor 4057. One of Arthur's knights

Coris 4058. Another of Arthur's knights

[Corneu]lans 468, 953. Cornishmen

Cor[neuale]is 121, 877; Corneualois 2545, 4122. Cornishmen

Cornot 3056, 3254, 3265. Cornishman

Cornouwalle 854, 1371, etc.; Cornoualle 1471, 2655, etc. Cornwall

Costentin 278. Constantine (emperor)

Costentin 2386. Constantine in Cornwall, Cotentin in Normandy, or perhaps a place-name chosen simply to make a point

Croiz Roge (la) 1909, 2419, etc.; la Croiz 1915, 1957. A cross marking a crossroads

Cuerlion. *See* Carloon

Damledé 909, 2584. The Lord God (*Dominus Deus*)

Denoalen 4382, 4434; also Denoalent 4374, Denoalan 4371, Denaalain 3474, Dinoalen 3484, Dinaalen 3484, Dono[a]len 3839, Donoalent 4238, Do[n]alan 4431, Danalain 3139. One of the three barons hostile to Tristran, who kills him

Deu 5, 755, etc.; Deus 22, 39, etc., Dé 804, 937, etc. God

Dinan 1085, 1133, 2847. Fief of Dinas

Dinas 1085, 1125, etc. Marc's seneschal and a friend of the lovers

Dureaume 2232; Durelme 4264. Durham (city in the North of England)

Escoce 3133. Scotland

Estiene, Saint 3070. St Stephen, the first Christian martyr

Evains 3483. Knight of the Round Table. *See* Ivain

Evrol, Saint 238. St Ebrulfus (Evroul), of Normandy, venerated at Bayeux

Frise 2246, 2408, 2610. Dumfries in Scotland (?)

Frocin 320, 645; also Frocins 328, Frocine 470, 1348, 1349. Dwarf and soothsayer at Marc's court, Tristran's enemy, killed by Marc for revealing his shameful secret

Gales 336, 2099, 2129. Wales

Galois 3758. Welshman

Gascoigne 1974. Gascony

Gauvain (Gawain) 3414, 3471; also Gauvains 3258, 3457, etc., Vauvain 4058. Arthur's nephew, knight of the Round Table

Gavoie 2631. Galloway in Scotland

Gerflet 3471, 4011, 4057; also Girflet 4014, Girflez 3259. Knight of the Round Table

Marie, Sainte 148, 1000. Mary, mother of Jesus

Martin, Saint 476. St Martin of Tours

Mont, le 2733. Presumably St Michael's Mount in the bay, off Marazion, in southwestern Cornwall

Morhot, le 136, 2038; also le Morhout 28, 848, 855, etc. An Irish giant, Iseut's uncle, who raided Cornwall for a tribute of Cornish children; slain by Tristran

Morrois 1648, 1662, 2090, etc.; also Morroi 1900, forest de Morrois 1275. Forest in southwestern Cornwall where the lovers take refuge for three years

Nicole 2879. Lincoln (birthplace of Andret, knight and counsellor at Marc's court)

Niques 4129. Nicaea

Noirs de la Montaigne, li 4016. The disguised Tristran, all in black, is taken for this legendary figure

Ogrin (also called *frere, l'ermite, maistre*) 1362, 2266, 2282, etc. The hermit having his oratory in the forest of Morrois

Orient 322. Orion

Orri 2818, 3017; also Orris 3019. Forester in the Morrois who shelters Tristran and Iseut

Otran 1406. Saracen King of Nîmes in the epic cycle of Guillaume d'Orange

Pas 3614. *See* Mal Pas

Passelande 3522. King Arthur's steed

Pentecoste, la 1776. The Feast of Pentecost

Perinis 2761, 2830, 3026, etc.; also Pirinis 764, 3393. Iseut's squire and messenger

Qeu (Kay) 3259. Knight of the Round Table and Arthur's seneschal

Renebors 3722. Ratisbonne/Regensburg

Richier, Saint 3466

Rome 281, 1138, 2386; also *la loi de Rome* (law of the Church of Rome) 660, 2194

Saisne 3254; also Sesne 3426. Saxon

Salemon 41, 1461. Solomon; two sayings are here attributed to him

Sanson, Saint 2973, 2994. Cathedral church of Lantyan, Marc's chief residence

Saut Tristran, le 954. Steep cliff in North Cornwall

Segoçon 279. Dwarf reputed to have been the lover of the Emperor Constantine's wife

Table Reonde, la 3379, 3706. Arthur's Round Table

Thomas, Saint 1126. St Thomas (presumably introduced for the rhyme)

Tintaguel 264, also Tintajol 880, 1040, 3150. A residence of King Marc, on the northwest coast of Cornwall, then near the Mal Pas

Tolas 4058. Knight of the Round Table

Tresmor, Saint 3076. St Trechmer/Trémeur, patron saint of the church of Carhaix (Caharés) in Brittany

Tristran 5, 18, 21, etc.; also Tristrain 407, Tristrans 467, 1423, 1637, Tristranz 2960. King Marc's nephew, and lover of Iseut

Tudele 3410. Tudela in Spanish Navarre

Urien 3483. Father of the knight Ivain

Vauvain 4058. Gauvain

Ylaire, Saint 4201. St Hilary

Yseut. *See* Iseut

Yvain. *See* Ivain